T0215325

Lecture Notes in Computer Science 12378

More information about this series at http://www.springer.com/series/7409

Eva Blomqvist · Paul Groth ·
Victor de Boer · Tassilo Pellegrini ·
Mehwish Alam · Tobias Käfer ·
Peter Kieseberg · Sabrina Kirrane ·
Albert Meroño-Peñuela ·
Harshvardhan J. Pandit (Eds.)

Semantic Systems

In the Era of Knowledge Graphs

16th International Conference on Semantic Systems, SEMANTiCS 2020
Amsterdam, The Netherlands, September 7–10, 2020
Proceedings

Springer

Editors
Eva Blomqvist
Linköping University
Linköping, Sweden

Victor de Boer
Department of Computer Science
Vrije Universiteit Amsterdam
Amsterdam, Noord-Holland,
The Netherlands

Mehwish Alam
FIZ Karlsruhe – Leibniz Institute for
Karlsruhe, Germany

Peter Kieseberg
UAS St. Pölten
St. Pölten, Niederösterreich, Austria

Albert Meroño-Peñuela
VU Amsterdam
Amsterdam, The Netherlands

Paul Groth
University of Amsterdam
Amsterdam, Noord-Holland,
The Netherlands

Tassilo Pellegrini
St. Pölten University of Applied Sciences
St. Pölten, Austria

Tobias Käfer
Karlsruhe Institute of Technology
Karlsruhe, Germany

Sabrina Kirrane
Vienna University of Economics
and Business
Vienna, Wien, Austria

Harshvardhan J. Pandit
ADAPT Centre
Trinity College Dublin
Dublin, Ireland

ISSN 0302-9743 ISSN 1611-3349 (electronic)
Lecture Notes in Computer Science
ISBN 978-3-030-59832-7 ISBN 978-3-030-59833-4 (eBook)
https://doi.org/10.1007/978-3-030-59833-4

LNCS Sublibrary: SL3 – Information Systems and Applications, incl. Internet/Web, and HCI

This Springer imprint is published by the registered company Springer Nature Switzerland AG
The registered company address is: Gewerbestrasse 11, 6330 Cham, Switzerland

Preface

This volume contains the proceedings of the 16th International Conference on Semantic Systems (SEMANTiCS 2020). SEMANTiCS offers a forum for the exchange of latest scientific results in semantic systems and complements these topics with new research challenges in areas like data science, machine learning, logic programming, content engineering, social computing, and the Semantic Web. The conference is in its 16th year and has developed into an internationally visible and professional event at the intersection of academia and industry. Contributors to and participants of the conference learn from top researchers and industry experts about emerging trends and topics in the wide area of semantic computing. The SEMANTiCS community is highly diverse; attendees have responsibilities in interlinking areas such as artificial intelligence, data science, knowledge discovery and management, big data analytics, e–commerce, enterprise search, technical documentation, document management, business intelligence, and enterprise vocabulary management.

The conference's subtitle in 2020 was "The Power of AI and Knowledge Graphs," and especially welcomed submissions to the following topics:

- Web Semantics and Linked (Open) Data
- Enterprise Knowledge Graphs, Graph Data Management, and Deep Semantics
- Machine Learning and Deep Learning Techniques
- Semantic Information Management and Knowledge Integration
- Terminology, Thesaurus, and Ontology Management
- Data Mining and Knowledge Discovery
- Reasoning, Rules, and Policies
- Natural Language Processing
- Data Quality Management and Assurance
- Explainable Artificial Intelligence
- Semantics in Data Science
- Semantics in Blockchain and Distributed Ledger Technologies
- Trust, Data Privacy, and Security with Semantic Technologies
- Economics of Data, Data Services, and Data Ecosystems

We additionally issued calls for three special tracks:

- Digital Humanities and Cultural Heritage
- Blockchain
- LegalTech

Due to the health crisis caused by the COVID-19 pandemic, SEMANTiCS 2020 took place in a highly reduced form. All on-site events were canceled and postponed to 2021. To keep a minimum level of continuity, the conference chairs decided to keep the call for scientific papers open and to publish a selection of reviewed papers as proceedings. The authors of accepted papers also provided a video presentation of their contribution, which was made available via the conference's website. In total, we received 36 submissions to the scientific call.

In order to properly provide high-quality reviews, a Program Committee (PC) comprising of 131 members supported us in selecting the papers with the highest impact and scientific merit. For each submission, at least four reviews were written independently from the assigned reviewers in a single–blind review process (author names are visible to reviewers, reviewers stay anonymous). After all reviews were submitted, the PC chairs compared the reviews and discussed discrepancies and different opinions with the reviewers to facilitate a meta–review and suggest a recommendation to accept or reject the paper. Overall, we accepted 8 papers which resulted in an acceptance rate of 22,2%.

We thank all authors who submitted papers and the PC for providing careful reviews in a quick turnaround time.

September 2020

Eva Blomqvist
Paul Groth
Victor de Boer
Tassilo Pellegrini
Mehwish Alam
Tobias Käfer
Peter Kieseberg
Sabrina Kirrane
Albert Meroño-Peñuela
Harshvardhan J. Pandit

Organization

Chairs and Program Committee of SEMANTICS 2020

Conference Chairs

Victor de Boer	Vrije Universiteit Amsterdam, The Netherlands
Tassilo Pellegrini	St. Pölten University of Applied Sciences, Austria

Research and Innovation Chairs

Eva Blomqvist	Linköping University, Sweden
Paul Groth	University of Amsterdam, The Netherlands

Special Track Chairs

Digital Humanities and Cultural Heritage

Mehwish Alam	FIZ Karlsruhe – Leibniz Institute for Information Infrastructure, Germany
Albert Merono	Vrije Universiteit Amsterdam, The Netherlands

Blockchain

Peter Kieseberg	St. Pölten University of Applied Sciences, Austria
Tobias Käfer	Karlsruhe Institute of Technology (KIT), Germany

LegalTech

Sabrina Kirrane	Vienna University of Economics and Business, Austria
Harshvadhan Pandit	ADAPT Centre, Ireland

Industry and Use Case Chairs

Christian Dirschl	Wolters Kluwer Deutschland GmbH, Germany
Marco Brattinga	Ordina, The Netherlands
Andreas Blumauer	Semantic Web Company, Austria

Poster and Demo Track Chairs

Maria Maleshkova	University of Bonn, Germany
Ilaria Tiddl	Vrije Universiteit Amsterdam, The Netherlands

Workshop and Satellite Events Chairs

Laura Daniele	TNO, The Netherlands
Tabea Tietz	FIZ Karlsruhe – Leibniz Institute for Information Infrastructure, Germany

Proceedings Chair

Victor de Boer | Vrije Universiteit Amsterdam, The Netherlands

Promotion Chairs

Thomas Thurner | Semantic Web Company, Austria
Julia Holze | AKSW, InfAI, Leipzig University, Germany
Stefan Summesberger | Plantsome Communication, Austria

Local Chairs

Catelijne Rauch-Blok | TNO, The Netherlands
Ronald Siebes | Vrije Universiteit Amsterdam, The Netherlands
Thomas Thurner | Semantic Web Company, Austria

Publicity Chair

Arjen Santema | The Netherlands Cadastre, Land Registry and Mapping Agency, The Netherlands

Permanent Advisory Board

Sören Auer | Fraunhofer, Germany
Andreas Blumauer | Semantic Web Company, Austria
Tobias Bürger | BMW Group, Germany
Christian Dirschl | Wolters Kluwer Deutschland GmbH, Germany
Victor de Boer | Vrije Universiteit Amsterdam, The Netherlands
Anna Fensel | Semantic Technology Institute (STI) Innsbruck, Austria
Dieter Fensel | Semantic Technology Institute (STI) Innsbruck, Austria
Mike Heininger | GfWM, Austria
Sebastian Hellmann | Leipzig University, Germany
Ute John | GfWM, Germany
Martin Kaltenböck | Semantic Web Company, Austria
Elmar Kiesling | TU Wien, Austria
Tassilo Pellegrini | St. Pölten University of Applied Sciences, Austria
Axel Polleres | Vienna University of Economics and Business, Austria
Felix Sasaki | DFKI, Germany
Harald Sack | FIZ Karlsruhe – Leibniz Institute for Information Infrastructure, Karlsruhe Institute of Technology (KIT), Germany

Program Committee - Research and Innovation Track and Special Tracks

Acosta Maribel | Karlsruhe Institute of Technology(KIT), Germany
Alam Mehwish | FIZ Karlsruhe – Leibniz Institute for Information Infrastructure, Karlsruhe Institute of Technology (KIT), Germany
Anelli Vito Walter | Politecnico di Bari, Italy
Asprino Luigi | University of Bologna and ISTC-CNR, Italy

Auer Sören   Leibniz University of Hannover, Germany
Aussenac-Gilles Nathalie   IRIT CNRS, France
Bischof Stefan   Siemens AG, Austria
Bobed Carlos   Everis, University of Zaragoza, Spain
Bonatti Piero   University of Naples Federico II, Italy
Bozzato Loris   Fondazione Bruno Kessler, Italy
Buil Aranda Carlos   Federico Santa Maria Technical University, Chile
Buitelaar Paul   Insight Centre for Data Analytics, National University
                                of Ireland Galway, Ireland
Casanovas Pompeu   Universitat Autònoma de Barcelona, Spain
Celino Irene   Cefriel, Italy
Ceolin Davide   Vrije Universiteit Amsterdam, The Netherlands
Champin Pierre-Antoine   LIRIS, Claude Bernard University Lyon 1, France
Chrysakis Ioannis   FORTH-ICS, Greece, and Ghent University, Belgium
Cimmino Arriaga   Andrea: Universidad Politécnica de Madrid, Spain
Ciuciu Ioana-Georgiana   Babes-Bolyai University of Cluj-Napoca, Romania
Corcho Oscar   Universidad Politécnica de Madrid, Spain
Daga Enrico   The Open University, UK
Daquino Marilena   University of Bologna, Italy
De Vos Marina   University of Bath, UK
Degeling Martin   Ruhr-Universität Bochum, Germany
Demidova Elena   L3S Research Center, Germany
Despres Sylvie   Laboratoire d'Informatique Médicale et de
                                BIOinformatique, France
Dietze Stefan   GESIS – Leibniz Institute for the Social Sciences,
                                Germany
Dimou Anastasia   Ghent University, Belgium
Ding Ying   The University of Texas at Austin, USA
Dirschl Christian   Wolters Kluwer Deutschland GmbH, Germany
Dojchinovski Milan   Czech Technical University in Prague, Czech Republic
Dörpinghaus Jens   Fraunhofer, Germany
Dragoni Mauro   Fondazione Bruno Kessler, Italy
Dumitrache Anca   Vrije Universiteit Amsterdam, The Netherlands
Eyharabide Victoria   STIH Laboratory, Sorbonne University, France
Färber Michael   Karlsruhe Institute of Technology (KIT), Germany
Faron Zucker Catherine   Université Nice Sophia Antipolis, France
Fathalla Said   University of Bonn, Germany
Feinerer Ingo   University of Applied Sciences Wiener Neustadt,
                                Austria
Fernández Javier D.   Roche, Switzerland
Filipowska Agata   Poznań University of Economics and Business, Poland
Freire Nuno   INESC-ID, Portugal
Gangemi Aldo   Università di Bologna, CNR-ISTC, Italy
Garcia Roberto   Universitat de Lleida, Spain
Garijo Daniel   University of Southern California, USA

Gol-Mohammadi Nazila	paluno - The Ruhr Institute for Software Technology, Germany
Gomez-Perez Jose Manuel	Expert System, Spain
Gray Alasdair	Heriot-Watt University, UK
Haase Peter	Metaphacts, Germany
Hammar Karl	Jönköping University, Sweden
Heling Lars	Karlsruhe Institute of Technology (KIT), Germany
Herder Eelco	Radboud University, The Netherlands
Heyvaert Pieter	Ghent University, Belgium
Hoekstra Rinke	University of Amsterdam, The Netherlands
Houben Geert-Jan	Delft University of Technology, The Netherlands
Huang Zhisheng	Vrije Universiteit Amsterdam, The Netherlands
Hyvönen Eero	Aalto University and University of Helsinki, Finland
Ibrahim Shimaa	University of Bonn, Germany
Jacobs Marc	Fraunhofer, Germany
Janev Valentina	Mihajlo Pupin Institute, Serbia
Käfer Tobias	Karlsruhe Institute of Technology (KIT), Germany
Kaffee Lucie-Aimée	University of Southampton, UK
Kannengießer Niclas	Karlsruhe Institute of Technology (KIT), Germany
Karam Naouel	Fraunhofer, Germany
Kärle Elias	STI-Innsbruck, Austria
Kauppinen Tomi	Aalto University School of Science, Finland
Kieseberg Peter	St. Pölten University of Applied Sciences, Austria
Kirrane Sabrina	Vienna University of Economics and Business, Austria
Kontokostas Dimitris	Leipzig University, Germany
Köpke Julius	Alpen-Adria-Universität Klagenfurt, Austria
Lange Christoph	Fraunhofer, RWTH Aachen University, Germany
Lefrançois Maxime	Ecole des Mines de Saint-Étienne, France
Lera Isaac	University of the Balearic Islands, Spain
Lioudakis Georgios	ICT abovo P.C., Greece
Lovrenčić Sandra	University of Zagreb, Croatia
Lully Vincent	Sorbonne University, France
Maccatrozzo Valentina	Vrije Universiteit Amsterdam, The Netherlands
Merkle Nicole	FZI Forschungszentrum Informatik, Germany
Meroño Peñuela Albert	Vrije Universiteit Amsterdam, The Netherlands
Montiel-Ponsoda Elena	Universidad Politécnica de Madrid, Spain
Moser Thomas	St. Pölten University of Applied Sciences, Austria
Nixon Lyndon	MODUL Technology GmbH, Austria
Nurgazina Jamilya	St. Pölten University of Applied Sciences, Austria
Obrst Leo	Mitre Corporation, USA
O'Sullivan Declan	Trinity College Dublin, Ireland
Padget Julian	University of Bath, UK
Palmirani Monica	CIRSFID, Italy
Pandit Harshvardhan J.	ADAPT Centre, Trinity College Dublin, Ireland
Paschke Adrian	Freie Universität Berlin, Germany
Paulheim Heiko	University of Mannheim, Germany

Pesquita Catia	LaSIGE, Universidade de Lisboa, Portugal
Pielorz Jasmin	Austrian Institute of Technology, Austria
Piras Luca	University of Brighton, UK
Potoniec Jędrzej	Poznań University of Technology, Poland
Pruski Cédric	Luxembourg Institute of Science and Technology, Luxembourg
Revenko Artem	Semantic Web Company GmbH, Austria
Rizzo Giuseppe	LINKS Foundation, Italy
Rodríguez Rocha	Oscar, Teach on Mars, France
Rodríguez-Doncel Víctor	Universidad Politécnica de Madrid, Spain
Sack Harald	FIZ Karlsruhe – Leibniz Institute for Information Infrastructure, Karlsruhe Institute of Technology (KIT), Germany
Schlobach Stefan	Vrije Universiteit Amsterdam, The Netherlands
Shvaiko Pavel	Trentino Digitale Spa, Italy
Silva Paulo	University of Coimbra, Portugal
Steyskal Simon	Siemens AG, Austria
Sure-Vetter York	Karlsruhe Institute of Technology(KIT), Germany
Taelman Ruben	Ghent University, Belgium
Tietz Tabea	FIZ Karlsruhe – Leibniz Institute for Information Infrastructure, Germany
Tiwari Sanju	Ontology Engineering Group, Spain
Todorov Konstantin	LIRMM, University of Montpellier, France
Tommasini Riccardo	University of Tartu, Estonia
Umbrich Jürgen	Vienna University of Economics and Business, Austria
Uren Victoria	Aston University, UK
Usbeck Ricardo	University of Paderborn, Germany
Van De Sompel Herbert	Data Archiving Networked Services, The Netherlands
van ErpMarieke	KNAW - Humanities Cluster, The Netherlands
Van Harmelen Frank	Vrije Universiteit Amsterdam, The Netherlands
Vander Sande Miel	Meemoo, Belgium
Vidal Maria Esther	Simon Bolivar University, Colombia
Villata Serena	CNRS, Signaux et Systèmes de Sophia-Antipolis, France
Waitelonis Joerg	yovisto GmbH, Germany
Wang Shenghui	University of Twente, The Netherlands
Wenning Rigo	World Wide Web Consortium, France
Wöß Wolfram	Johannes Kepler University Linz, Austria

Additional Reviewers

Bartscherer Frederic	Karlsruhe Institute of Technology (KIT), Germany
Cano Benito Juan	Universidad Politécnica de Madrid, Spain
Heba Mohamed	.
Kuculo Tin	L3S Research Center, Germany

Marinucci Ludovica	Institute for Cognitive Sciences and Technologies (ISTC), Italy
Papadopoulos Petros	Heriot-Watt University, UK
Saier Tarek	Karlsruhe Institute of Technology (KIT), Germany
Scrocca Mario	Cefriel, Italy

Contents

The New DBpedia Release Cycle: Increasing Agility and Efficiency
in Knowledge Extraction Workflows   1
   Marvin Hofer, Sebastian Hellmann, Milan Dojchinovski,
   and Johannes Frey

DBpedia Archivo: A Web-Scale Interface for Ontology Archiving Under
Consumer-Oriented Aspects   19
   Johannes Frey, Denis Streitmatter, Fabian Götz, Sebastian Hellmann,
   and Natanael Arndt

A Knowledge Retrieval Framework for Household Objects and Actions
with External Knowledge   36
   Alexandros Vassiliades, Nick Bassiliades, Filippos Gouidis,
   and Theodore Patkos

Semantic Annotation, Representation and Linking of Survey Data   53
   Felix Bensmann, Andrea Papenmeier, Dagmar Kern, Benjamin Zapilko,
   and Stefan Dietze

QueDI: From Knowledge Graph Querying to Data Visualization   70
   Renato De Donato, Martina Garofalo, Delfina Malandrino,
   Maria Angela Pellegrino, Andrea Petta, and Vittorio Scarano

EcoDaLo: Federating Advertisement Targeting with Linked Data   87
   Sven Lieber, Ben De Meester, Ruben Verborgh, and Anastasia Dimou

MINDS: A Translator to Embed Mathematical Expressions Inside
SPARQL Queries   104
   Damien Graux, Gezim Sejdiu, Claus Stadler, Giulio Napolitano,
   and Jens Lehmann

Integrating Historical Person Registers as Linked Open Data
in the WarSampo Knowledge Graph   118
   Mikko Koho, Petri Leskinen, and Eero Hyvönen

Author Index   127

The New DBpedia Release Cycle: Increasing Agility and Efficiency in Knowledge Extraction Workflows

Marvin Hofer[1]([envelope]) [iD], Sebastian Hellmann[1], Milan Dojchinovski[1,2] [iD], and Johannes Frey[1]

[1] Knowledge Integration and Language Technologies (KILT/AKSW), DBpedia Association/InfAI, Leipzig University, Leipzig, Germany
{hofer,hellmann,dojchinovski,frey}@informatik.uni-leipzig.de
[2] Web Intelligence Research Group, FIT, Czech Technical University in Prague, Prague, Czech Republic
milan.dojchinovski@fit.cvut.cz

Abstract. Since its inception in 2007, DBpedia has been constantly releasing open data in RDF, extracted from various Wikimedia projects using a complex software system called the DBpedia Information Extraction Framework (DIEF). For the past 12 years, the software received a plethora of extensions by the community, which positively affected the size and data quality. Due to the increase in size and complexity, the release process was facing huge delays (from 12 to 17 months cycle), thus impacting the agility of the development. In this paper, we describe the new DBpedia release cycle including our innovative release workflow, which allows development teams (in particular those who publish large, open data) to implement agile, cost-efficient processes and scale up productivity. The DBpedia release workflow has been re-engineered, its new primary focus is on *productivity* and *agility*, to address the challenges of size and complexity. At the same time, *quality* is assured by implementing a comprehensive testing methodology. We run an experimental evaluation and argue that the implemented measures increase agility and allow for cost-effective quality-control and debugging and thus achieve a higher level of maintainability. As a result, DBpedia now publishes regular (i.e. monthly) releases with over 21 billion triples with minimal publishing effort.

Keywords: DBpedia · Knowledge extraction · Data publishing · Quality assurance

1 Introduction

Since its inception in 2007, the DBpedia project [8] has been continuously releasing large, open datasets, extracted from Wikimedia projects such as Wikipedia and Wikidata [15]. The data has been extracted using a complex software

---

Sebastian Hellmann—https://global.dbpedia.org/id/3eGWH.

system known as the DBpedia Information Extraction Framework (DIEF). Over the past years the system has received a plethora of extensions and fixes by the community which resulted in creating monolithic releases.

Until 2017, The DBpedia release process has been primarily focused on *data quality* and *size*, however, it neglected other two important and desirable goals: *productivity* and *agility* (cf. [3] for balancing the magic triangle on quality, productivity and agility The release process was facing massive delays (from 12 to 17 months) with increasing costs of development and lower productivity due to the sole focus on quality and the increased size and complexity. The releases were so large and complex that the DBpedia core team failed to produce them for almost three years (2017–2019). Note that this was not a performance nor scalability related issue. The DBpedia release workflow has been re-engineered, its new primary focus is on *productivity* and *agility*, to address the challenges of size and complexity. At the same time, the *quality* aspects are assured by implementing a comprehensive testing methodology.

In this paper, we describe the new DBpedia release cycle including our innovative release workflow, which allows development teams (in particular those who publish large, open data) to implement agile, cost-effective processes and scale up productivity. As a result of our innovation DBpedia now produces over 21 billion triples per month with minimal publishing effort.

The paper is organized as follows. First, in Sect. 2, we summarize the two biggest challenges as a motivation for our work, followed by an overview of the release workflow described in Sect. 3. The main process innovations and conceptual design principles are described in Sect. 4. The implemented testing methodology is described in Sect. 5 and the results from several experiments showing the impact, capabilities and the gain from the new release cycle are presented in Sect. 6. Section 7 reports on technologies that relate to ours. Finally, Sect. 8 concludes the paper and presents future work directions.

2   Background and Motivation

1. Agility. Data quality is one of the largest and oldest topics in computer science independent of current trends such as Big Data or Knowledge Graphs and has a vast amount of facets to consider [16]. Data quality, often defined as *"fitness for use"*, poses many challenges that are frequently neglected or delayed in the software engineering process of applications until the very end, i.e. when the application is demonstrated to the end-user. In this paper, we will refer to this phase of the process as the *"point-of-truth"* since it marks an important transition of **data** (transferred between machines and software) to **information**. At this point, results are presented in a human-readable form so that humans can evaluate them according to their current knowledge and reasoning capacity. We argue that any delay or late manifestation of such a *"point-of-truth"* impacts cost-effectiveness of data quality management and stands in direct contradiction to the first and other principles of the agile manifesto: "Our highest priority is to satisfy the customer through early and continuous delivery of valuable software."

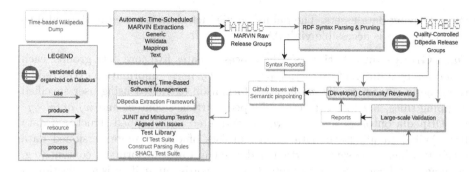

Fig. 1. The DBpedia release cycle.

[2]. Our release cycle counteracts the delay by introducing frequent, fixed time-based releases in combination with automated delivery of data to applications via the DBpedia Databus (cf. Subsect. 4.1).

2. Efficiency. We focus on efficiency as a major factor of productivity. Data quality follows the Law of Diminishing Returns [11] (similar to Pareto-Efficiency or 80/20 rule), meaning that initially decent quality can be achieved quickly, while complex errors become increasingly much harder to find and fix, up to a point where adding more resources (e.g. human labor or development power) produces similar or worse results[1]. In our experience, there is **no exception to the law of diminishing returns in data**. It affects all data projects, be they collaboratively edited such as Wikidata, semi-automatic such as DBpedia or fully automated machine learning approaches. Additionally, **data quality does usually not depend primarily on the effort invested (e.g. by a large community) but on the efficiency of the development process and the ability to effectively improve data in a sustainable manner.** Measures to increase efficiency are traceability of errors (Subsect. 4.2) combined with testing (Sect. 5).

3   DBpedia Release Cycle Overview

The DBpedia release cycle is a time-driven release process triggered on a regular basis (i.e. monthly). The DIEF framework (in a distributed computational environment) is executed and data is extracted on the latest Wikipedia dump. The basis of the release cycle relies on the **DBpedia Databus platform**, which acts as a data publishing middleware and is responsible for maintaining information about published data by organizing collection of files as groups and artifacts. The DBpedia Databus is the core component which helps data publishers to publish and promote their data, additionally, it supports data consumers in searching

---

[1] Meaning overall less output per unit.

and retrieving data assets. The published file metadata is stored in the Databus repository and is accessible via SPARQL.

Data Groups and Artifacts. The process creates five core data groups, each generated by a different extraction process[2]: *i) generic*–information extracted by the generic extractors, *ii) mappings*–information extracted using user specified mapping rules, *iii) text*–extracted Wikipedia article's content and *iv) ontology*– the DBpedia ontology and *v) wikidata*–extracted and mapped structured data from Wikidata [6]. Each data group consists of one or more versioned data artifacts which represent a particular dataset in different formats, content (e.g. language) and compression variants. In other words, an artifact is a collection of multiple files, which can be addressed with a unique Databus identifier. The artifact IRIs have hierarchical structure and follow a pattern. For example: https:// databus.dbpedia.org/dbpedia/mappings/instance-types/2020.04.01.

Where 'dbpedia' refers to a publisher, 'mappings' refers to a group, 'instance-types' refers to an artifact and '2020.04.01' refers to its version.

Publishing Agents. A publishing agent acts on behalf of a person or organization and publishes data on the Databus. A Databus account is created and assigned to each agent. The initial set of data groups are published on the Databus by the MARVIN publishing agent.[3] In addition to the MARVIN agent, there is also the DBpedia agent, which publishes cleaned data artifacts, i.e. syntactically valid. The configuration files used to generate the MARVIN and DBpedia releases are available as a public git repository.[4]

Cleansing, Validation and Reporting. The data (i.e., triples) published by the MARVIN agent is then picked up and parsed by the DBpedia agent to create strictly valid RDF triples without any violations (including warnings and errors) based on Apache Jena[5]. Finally, syntactically cleaned data artifacts are published by the DBpedia agent. While the data is syntactically valid, other data quality issues might persist. For example, the IRIs of particular subjects, predicates and objects do not conform to a predefined schema, the data can be structurally incorrect and does not conform to the ontology restrictions, or the release might be incomplete (e.g. missing artifacts). A large-scale validation is done for each release and the error reports are delivered to the community for a review. Figure 1 depicts the overall DBpedia data release cycle.

The complete new DBpedia release approach has been deployed in February 2020. Releases are created every month, except the *text* group, which is released every three months, due to its complexity. We have deployed a light-weight dashboard (see http://release-dashboard.dbpedia.org/) which summarizes the releases, including the extraction process progress, extraction logs and overall statistics. Table 1 provides statistics for different DBpedia data groups for three

---

[2] https://databus.dbpedia.org/dbpedia/.

[3] https://databus.dbpedia.org/marvin/.

[4] https://git.informatik.uni-leipzig.de/dbpedia-assoc/marvin-config.

[5] https://jena.apache.org.

Table 1. Size metrics (i.e. triples count) for DBpedia data groups and release periods.

Version	Generic	Mappings	Text	Wikidata
2016.10.01	4,524,347,267	730,221,071	9,282,719,317	738,329,191
2019.08.30	4,109,424,594	953,187,791	-	-
2020.04.01	3,736,165,682	1,075,837,576	11,200,431,258	4,998,301,802

releases; from Oct 2016,[6] Aug 2019[7] and Apr 2020.[8] '2016.10.01' is the last monolithic legacy release, which we added for comparability. Note that we do not provide numbers for 'text' and 'wikidata' data groups for the '2019.08.30' due to the incompleteness of these releases.

The numbers from Table 1 show that the amount of triples in the 'mappings', 'text' and 'wikidata' data groups is constantly increasing over time. By contrast, the 'generic' data group provides less triples. This is primarily due to the strict testing procedures which have been put in place and as a consequence, invalid statements have been not included in the release. Note that the numbers are also impacted by the configuration of the DIEF system (e.g. enabled extractors) for different releases. Compared to the Wikidata statistic,[9] the DBpedia 'wikidata' extraction produces five times the amount of statements published by itself, mainly because of reification and materialization processes during the extraction (e.g. transitive instance types).

4 Conceptual Design Principles

Two design principles have driven the design and implementation of the new DBpedia release cycle: *i) time-driven data releases* enable more frequent and regular DBpedia releases, and *ii) traceability and issue management* enables more efficient linking of issues with tests and tracking their causes.

4.1 Time-Driven vs. Quality-Driven Data Releases

While many of the principles of the agile manifesto are applicable, the most relevant principle "Working software is the primary measure of progress" [2] can not be applied directly to data. As motivated in Sect. 2, the judgment of whether "data works" is withheld until the *"point-of-truth"* on the customer/end-user side. From our own past experience and from conversations with related development teams, it is a fallacy that the developer or data publisher has the capacity to evaluate when "data is useful", following their own quality-driven or feature-driven agenda. Since adopting an attitude of *"quality creep"*[10] bears the risk of

---

[6] https://databus.dbpedia.org/vehnem/collections/dbpedia-2016-10-01.
[7] https://databus.dbpedia.org/vehnem/collections/dbpedia-2019-08-30.
[8] https://databus.dbpedia.org/vehnem/collections/dbpedia-2020-04-01.
[9] https://tools.wmflabs.org/wikidata-todo/stats.php.
[10] Analogous to feature creep in software.

delaying releases and prevent data reaching end-users with valuable feedback, we decided to switch to a strict time-based schedule for releasing following these principles:

1. Automated Schedule vs. Self-discipline. Releases are fully automated via the MARVIN extraction robot. This alleviates developers from the decision when "data is ready". Else extensive testing of data might have an adverse effect. Developers are prone to "fixing one more bug" instead of delivering data for proper end-user feedback.

2. Subordination of Software. The whole software development cycle is completely subordinate to the data release cycle with time-driven, automatic check-out of the tested master branch.

3. Automated Delivery. Data is published on the DBpedia Databus, which allows subscription for data (artifacts/versions/files), which in term enables auto-updated application deployment[11] and therefore facilitating point-of-truth feedback opportunities earlier and continuously.

4.2 Traceability and Issue Management

Any data issues discovered at the point-of-truth start a costly process of back-tracking the error in reverse order of the pipeline that delivered it. The problem of tracing and fixing errors becomes even more complicated in Extract-Transform-Load (ETL) procedures where the data is heavily manipulated and/or aggregated from different sources. A quintessential ETL example is the DBpedia system, which implements sophisticated ETL procedures for extraction and refinement of data from semi-structured mixed-quality and crowd-sourced sources such as Wikipedia and Wikidata. Over the years, a huge community of users and contributors has formed around DBpedia, that are reporting errors via different communication channels such as Slack, Github and the DBpedia forum. A vast majority of the issues are associated with i) a piece of data and ii) a procedure (i.e. code) which has generated the data. In the past, the management of issues has been done in an ad-hoc manner. Recently, we introduced a systematic, test-driven approach for managing data and code-related issues using Linked Data. In order to enable more efficient traceability and management of issues, we have introduced two technical improvements:

1. Explicit Association of Data Artifacts and Code. Previously DBpedia was grouped by language, which made backtracking difficult. Now every created and published data artifact is explicitly associated, due to a one-time manual mapping, with the procedure (i.e. code) which created the artifact. For example, the "instance-types"[12] artifact is associated with the "MappingExtractor.scala" class which created the artifact ("View code" action on the Databus website)

---

[11] via Docker, out of scope for this paper, see https://wiki.dbpedia.org/develop/datasets/latest-core-dataset-releases.

[12] https://databus.dbpedia.org/dbpedia/mappings/instance-types/2020.04.01.

This allows for easier tracking of errors and relates data to code. A query[13] on http://databus.dbpedia.org/sparql revealed that 26 code references exist and 12 are still missing for the wikidata group.

2. **Semantic Pinpointing for Issue Management.** A major difficulty for tackling data issues was to identify in which file and version the error occurred. Team-internal discussions as well as submitted community issues did not have the proper vocabulary to describe the datasets, exactly. Using Databus identifiers, these errors can be pinpointed to the exact artifact, version and file.

Table 2. Testing methodology levels.

Level	Method	Description
Software	JUnit	Functional software tests on data parsers and extractor methods
Constructs	Custom rules	IRI patterns and encoding errors, datatype and literal conformity and vocabulary usage
Syntax	Syntax parsing	Syntax parsing of output files implemented with Jena with customized selection of applicable errors and warnings
Shapes	SHACL	A mix of auto-generated and custom SHACL test suites for domain and value range, cardinality and graph structure
Integration	SPARQL over metadata	Verifies completeness of the releases and overall changes of quality metrics using Databus file/package metadata
Consumer	SPARQL on graph	Use case and domain specific SPARQL queries at consumer side. Point-of-truth evaluation

3. **Test-Driven Approach for Issue Management (Minidump).** Testing was mostly done after publishing (post-release) and reported issues were often ignored as reproduction of the error were either untraceable or required a full extraction (weeks) and difficult manual intervention. We created a test suite library that can be executed post-release as well as on small-scale, extendable Wikipedia XML dump samples (collection of Wikipedia pages), producing a small release, i.e. a minidump. Tests on this minidump are executed on git push via continuous integration (minutes), thus enabling the following workflow: 1. for each reported data issue, a representative entity is chosen and added to the minidump. 2. a specific test at the appropriate level (see next section) is devised.

---

[13] https://git.informatik.uni-leipzig.de/dbpedia-assoc/marvin-config/-/tree/master/paper-supplement/codelink.

3. the code is improved so that the test passes. 4. post-release the same test is executed to check whether the fix was successful at larger scale, also testing for side-effects or breaking other parts of the software.

5   Testing Methodology

To cover the entire DBpedia knowledge management life cycle, from software development and debugging to release quality checks, we implemented a robust "Testing Methodology" divided into six different levels listed in Table 2. The first level affects software development only. The following three levels (Constructs, Syntax, and Shapes) are executed on the minidump as well as on the full releases. In comparison, the legacy extraction process did include tests but only covered the testing aspects of the Software and Syntax layers. The continuously updated developer wiki[14] explains in detail, which steps are necessary to 1. add Construct and SHACL tests, 2. extend the minidumps with entities, 3. configure the Apache Jena-based parser and 4. run the tests and find related code. Besides the improvement in efficiency, the levels of testing were extended to cope with the variety of issues submitted to the DBpedia Issue tracker[15].

```
trigger:dbpedia_ontology   a   cv:IRI_Trigger ;
    rdfs:label     "DBpedia Ontology IRIs trigger" ;
    cvt:pattern   "^http://dbpedia.org/ontology/.*" .
validator:dbpedia_ontology a   cv:IRI_Validator ;
    rdfs:label      "DBpedia Ontology validator" ;
    cvv:oneOfVocab <dbpedia/ontology/dbo-snapshots.nt> .
<#dbpediaOntology>   a   cv:TestGenerator ;
    cv:trigger    trigger:dbpedia_ontology ;
    cv:validator validator:dbpedia_ontology .
```

Listing 1: Test case covering the correct use of the DBpedia ontology.

5.1   Construct Validation

To investigate the layout and encoding conformity of produced data, we introduce an approach that focuses on the in-depth validation of its pre-syntactical constructs. This concept differs from *Syntactical Validation*, since it does not rely on the complete syntactical correctness of the analyzed data, but checks the conformity for its single constructs. A construct can be any character or byte sequence inside a data serialization, typically a specific part in the EBNF grammar [12]. In the case of RDF NTriples and DBpedia, interesting constructs are IRIs or literals represented by the subject, predicate, or object part of a single triple. Blank nodes are ignored as they follow unpredictable patterns. Moreover,

---

[14] http://dev.dbpedia.org/Improve_DBpedia.
[15] https://github.com/dbpedia/extraction-framework/issues?q=is%3Aissue+is%3Aopen+label\%3Aci-tests.

a single construct can be validated independently of inaccuracies in the rest of the data. This method can be used to gain better test coverage metrics over specific data parts, such as IRI patterns in RDF.

Assessing layout quality of an IRI is motivated by:

1. Linked Data HTTP requests are more lenient towards variation. RDF and SPARQL are strict and require exact match. Especially it is relevant that each release uses the exact same IRIs as before, which is normally not handled in syntactical parsing.
2. optional percent-encoding, especially for international chars and gen/sub-delims[16] = '!', '\$', '&', ''', '(', ')', '*', '+', ',', ';', '='
3. Valid IRIs with wrong namespace **http**://www.wikidata.org/**entity**/Q64 or **https**://www.wikidata.org/**wiki**/Q64 or wrong layout (e.g. wkd:QQ64)
4. Correct use of vocabulary and correct linking

Complementary to *Syntactical Validation*, this approach provides a more fine-grained quality assessment methodology and can be specified as follows:

Construct Test Trigger: A *Construct Trigger* describes a pattern (e.g., a regular expression or wildcard) that covers groups of constructs (i.e. namepsaces for IRIs) and assigns them to several domain-specific test cases. Moreover, if a trigger matches a given construct, then it triggers several validation methods that were assigned by a test generator. These patterns are highly flexible, and it is possible to define overlapping triggers.

Construct Validator: To verify a group of triggered constructs, a *Construct Validator* describes a specific reusable test approach. Several conformity constraints are currently implemented: *regex* - regular expression matching, *oneOf* - matching a static string, *oneOfVocab* - is contained in the ontology or vocabulary, and *doesNotContain* - does not contain a specific sequence. Further, we implemented generic RDF validators, based on Apache Jena, to test the syntactical correctness of single IRI and literal constructs.

Construct Test Generator: A construct test generator defines an $1 : n$ relation between a *Construct Trigger* and several *Construct Validators* to describe a set of test cases.

For our approach, it was convenient to use Apache Spark and line-based regular expressions on NTriples to fetc.h these specific constructs. Listing 1 outlines an example construct test case specification covering DBpedia ontology IRIs, by checking the correct use of defined *owl:Class*, *owl:Datatype*, and *owl:ObjectProperties*. The *Construct Validation* approach seems theoretically extensible to validate namespaces, identifiers, attributes, layouts and encodings in other data formats like XML, CSV, JSON as well. However, we had no proper use case to justify the effort to explore it.

---

[16] https://tools.ietf.org/html/rfc3987.

5.2   Syntactical Validation

The procedure of *Syntax Validation* verifies the conformity of a serialized data format with its defined grammar. Normally, RDF parsers distinguish between different levels of"syntactical correctness", including errors and warnings. Errors represent entirely fraudulent statements, in the sense of irreproducible information, and a warning refers to an incorrect format of e.g., a datatype literal.

It is important to validate and clean the produced output of the DIEF, since some of the used methods are bloated, deprecated and erroneous. Therefore, the used *Syntax Validation* is configured to remove all statements containing warnings or errors. This guarantees better interoperability in the target software, which might use parsers considering some warnings as errors. The parser is a wrapper around Apache Jena, highly parallelized and is configured as fault-tolerant to skip erroneous triples and log exceptions correctly. The syntax cleaning process produces strictly valid RDF NTriples, on the one hand, and generates RDF syntax error reports, on the other. The original file is also kept on MARVIN to allow later inspection. The error reports provide structured input for community-driven and automated feedback. Finally, the valid NTriples are sorted to remove duplicated statements. This can later be utilized to compare iterations or modified versions of specific data releases.

5.3   Shape Validation

SHACL (Shapes Constraint Language)[17] is a W3C Recommendation which defines a language for validating RDF graphs against a set of conditions. These conditions are provided as shapes and other constructs expressed in the form of an RDF graph. SHACL is used within DBpedia's knowledge extraction and release process to validate and evaluate the results (i.e. generated RDF). The defined SHACL tests are executed against the extracted minidump results (Subsect. 4.2).

```
<#Český_(rozcestník)_cs> a sh:NodeShape ;
  sh:targetNode <http://cs.dbpedia.org/resource/Český_(rozcestník)> ;
  # assuring that the disambiguation extractor for Czech is active
  # notice that for some languages the disambiguation extractor is not
  ↪ active (e.g. the case Czech)
  sh:property [
    sh:path dbo:wikiPageDisambiguates ;
    sh:hasValue <http://cs.dbpedia.org/resource/Český> ;
  ] .
```

Listing 2: SHACL test for existence of Czech disambiguation links.

---

[17] Edited by D. Kontokostas, the former CTO of DBpedia: https://www.w3.org/TR/shacl/.

Motivating Example. Recently, the Czech DBpedia community identified that the disambiguation links have not been extracted for Czech. The lack was discovered by an application-specific integration test (next section). Upon fixing the problem (configuration-related), a SHACL test (Listing 5.3) was implemented which will in future detect non-existence of the "disambiguation links" dataset on commit by checking a representative triple.

5.4 Integration Validation

Since software and artifacts possess a high coherence and loose coupling, additional methods are necessary to ensure overall quality control. To validate the completeness of a final DBpedia release, we run SPARQL queries on the Databus graph in order to check if all expected files are found. Listing 3 shows an example query to acquire an overview of the completeness of the mappings group releases on the DBpedia Databus.[18] Other application-specific tests exists, e.g. DBpedia Spotlight needs 3 specific files to compute a language model.[19]

6 Experimental Evaluation

Section 3 and Table 1 has already introduced and discussed the size of the new releases. For our experiments, we used the versions listed there and in addition the MARVIN pre-release.

```
SELECT ?expected ?actual ?delta ?versionStr ?versionIRI {
  {SELECT ?expected (COUNT(DISTINCT ?distribution) AS ?actual)
        ((?actual-?expected) AS ?delta) ?versionIRI ?versionString {
    VALUES (?artifact ?expected) {
      ( mapp:geo-coordinates-mappingbased 29 )
      ( mapp:instance-types 80 )
      ( mapp:mappingbased-literals 40 )
      ( mapp:mappingbased-objects 120 )
      ( mapp:specific-mappingbased-properties 40 )
  }
    ?dataset dataid:artifact ?artifact .
    ?dataset dataid:version ?versionIRI .
    ?dataset dcat:distribution ?distribution . }
  }
  FILTER(?delta != 0)
} ORDER BY DESC(?versionStr)
```

Listing 3: SPARQL integration test comparing expected file counts of artifacts with the actually released number.

---

[18] All groups https://git.informatik.uni-leipzig.de/dbpedia-assoc/marvin-config/-/tree/master/test.

[19] SPARQL query at https://forum.dbpedia.org/t/tasks-for-volunteers/163 Languages with missing redirects/disambiguations.

As a variety of methods (e.g. [7], a pre-cursor of SHACL) has been evaluated on DBpedia before and is not repeated here. We focused this evaluation on the novel *Construct Validation*, which introduce a whole previously invisible error class. Results are summarized, detailed reports will be linked to the Databus artifacts in the future. For this paper, they are archived here.[20]

Construct Validation Tests. To validate the constructs of the triples produced by DIEF, we specified generic and custom domain-specific test cases. With respect to the constructs in Subsect. 5.1, we provide different test cases for IRI compliance and literal conformity to increase the test coverage over the extracted data. The IRI test cases focus on the encoding or layout of an IRI, and check the correct use of several vocabularies. In case of extracted DBpedia instance IRIs, the test cases validate the correctness considering that a DBpedia resource IRIs should not include sequences of '?', '#', '[', ']', '%21', '%24', '%26', '%27', '%28', '%29', '%2A', '%2B', '%2C', '%3B', '%3D' inside the segment part and follows Wikipedia conventions. The vocabulary test cases, which will be automated later, include tests for these schemas:[21] dbo, foaf, geo, rdf, rdfs, xsd, itsrdf, and skos to ensure the use of the respective ontology or vocabulary specification. Further, generic IRI and literal test cases are implemented to test their syntactical correctness and to validate the lexical format of typed literals. The full collection of specified custom *Construct Validation* test cases is versioned at the DIEF git repository.[22]

Construct Validation Metrics. We define *Construct Validation Metrics* to measure the error rate and the overall test coverage for IRI patterns, encoding errors, datatype formats and vocabularies used in the produced data. The overall construct test coverage is defined by dividing the number of constructs that at least trigger one test by the total amount of found constructs.

Coverage := Triggered Constructs / Total Constructs

The overall error rate (in percent) is determined by dividing the number of constructs that have at least one error by the total number of covered constructs.

Error Rate := Erroneous Constructs / Covered Constructs

Test Results. The custom tests for the DBpedia 'generic' and 'mappings' release have an average of 87% IRI coverage (cf. Table 3). The test coverage can be increased by writing more custom test cases, but concerning the 80/20 rule, this could result in high efforts and the missing IRI patterns are presumably used inside of homepage or external link relations. The new strict syntax cleaning was introduced on the '2019.08.30' version of the mappings release and later applied to the 'generic' release. It removes a significant amount of IRIs from the 'generic' version (~500 million) and only a fraction from the 'mappings' release, reflecting the different extraction quality of them both. Although strict parsing

---

[20] https://git.informatik.uni-leipzig.de/dbpedia-assoc/marvin-config/-/tree/master/paper-supplement/reports.

[21] http://prefix.cc.

[22] https://github.com/dbpedia/extraction-framework/blob/master/dump/src/test/resources/dbpedia-specific-ci-tests.ttl.

Table 3. Custom *Construct Validation* test statistics of the DBpedia and MARVIN release for the generic and mappings group (Gr). Displaying the total IRI counts, the *Construct Validation* test coverage of IRIs, and construct errors (e.g. wrong IRI pattern or vocab usage) of certain Databus releases.

Gr.	Release	Version	IRIs total	Coverage	Errors	Error rate
Generic	DBpedia	2016.10.01	12,228,978,594	83.93%	15,823,204	0.15%
	MARVIN	2019.08.30	11,089,492,791	90.98%	18,113,408	0.18%
	DBpedia	2019.08.30	11,089,492,791	90.98%	18,113,408	0.18%
	MARVIN	2020.04.01	10,527,299,298	89.59%	18,662,921	0.20%
	DBpedia	2020.04.01	10,022,095,645	89.32%	18,652,958	0.21%
Mappings	DBpedia	2016.10.01	2,058,288,765	84.01%	6,692,902	0.39%
	MARVIN	2019.08.30	2,686,427,646	85.99%	6,951,976	0.30%
	DBpedia	2019.08.30	2,678,475,356	86.01%	6,875,930	0.30%
	MARVIN	2020.04.01	3,020,660,756	86.24%	7,514,376	0.29%
	DBpedia	2020.04.01	3,019,942,481	86.24%	7,505,332	0.29%

was used and invalid triples are removed, the other errors remain, which we consider a good indicator that the *Construct Validation* is complementary to syntax parsing.

Table 4 shows four independent *Construct Validation* test cases.

XSD Date Literal (xdt). This generic triple test validates the correct format use of xsd:date typed literals (`"yyyy-mm-dd"^^xsd:date`). Due to the use of strict syntax cleaning, as shown in Table 4, subsequent release later than '2016.10.01' do not contain incorrectly formatted date type literals, loosing several million triples. Removing warnings leads to better interoperability later.

RDF Language String (lang). The DIEF uses particular serialization methods to create triples that are often duplicated and contain deprecated code fragments. The post-processing module had an issue to build correct `rdf:langString` serializations by adding this IRI as explicit datatype instead of the language tag. Considering the N-Triples specification, this is an implicit literal datatype assigned by their language tags. This bug was not recognized by later parsers (i.e. Apache Jena), because the produced statements are syntactically correct. Therefore, to cover this behavior we introduce a generic test case for this kind of literals. The prevalence of this test is described by the pattern '`"*"^^rdf:langString`' and the test validation is defined by an assertion that the pattern should not exist. Moreover, if a construct can be tested, the test directly fails and so the prevalence of the test is equal to its errors. A post-processing bug fix was provided before the '2020.04.01' release, and considering Table 4 was solved properly.

Table 4. *Construct Validation* results of the four test cases: XSD date literal (xdt), RDF language string (lang), DBpedia ontology (dbo) and DBpedia Instance URIs which contain a question mark (dbrq). We mention the total number of triggered constructs (prevalence), the aggregated amount of errors, and the percentile error rate.

Gr.	Test	Version	Prevalence	Errors	Error rate
DBp. generic	xdt	2016.10.01	32,104,814	4,419,311	13.77%
		2019.08.30	28,193,951	0	0%
		2020.04.01	26,193,711	0	0%
	lang	2016.10.01	229,009,107	229,009,107	100%
		2019.08.30	353,220,047	353,220,047	100%
		2020.04.01	0	0	0%
DBp. mappings	dbo	2016.10.01	419,745,660	6,686,707	1.594%
		2019.08.30	496,841,363	6,857,202	1.381%
		2020.04.01	567,570,166	7,500,707	1.322%
	dbrq	2016.10.01	853,927,831	0	0%
		2019.08.30	1,198,382,078	15,407	0.001286%
		2020.04.01	1,354,209,107	0	0%

DBpedia Ontology URIs (dbo). To cover correct use of correct vocabularies, some ontology test cases are specified. For the DBpedia ontology this test is assigned to the 'http://dbpedia.org/ontology/*' namespace and checks for correctly used IRIs of the DBpedia ontology. The test demonstrates that the used DBpedia ontology instances used inside the three 'mappings' release versions do not conform with the DBpedia ontology (cf. Table 4). By inspecting this in detail, we discovered the intensive production of a non-defined class dbo:Location, which is pending to be fixed. Error rate is lower in later releases, as size increased.

DBpedia Instance URIs (dbrq). This test case checks one encoding criterion of extracted DBpedia resource IRIs. Therefore, if a construct matches 'http://[a-z\-]*.dbpedia.org/resource/*' the last path segment is checked not to contain the '?' symbol as this kind of IRIs should never carry a query part. As displayed in Table 4, the incorrect extraction of the dbr IRIs considering the '?' symbol occurred for version '2019.08.30' and was then solved in later releases.

Test Coverage of Non-DBpedia Datasets. To show the re-usability of the *Construct Validation* approach, we analyzed a set of external RDF datasets.[23] For these datasets our custom test cases achieved an average coverage around 10%. (cf. Table 5). The biggest part is covered by the custom vocabulary tests, especially foaf, rdf, rdfs and skos are commonly used across multiple RDF datasets. Another useful test case represents the correct use of DBpedia IRIs inside these datasets (inbound links). Almost in all external datasets, it could be recognized that backlinked DBpedia instances or ontology IRIs are wrong

---

[23] https://databus.dbpedia.org/vehnem/collections/construct-validation-input.

Table 5. Custom *Construct Validation* statistics and triple counts of external RDF NTriples releases on the Databus. Including IRI test coverage and the number of failed tests based on the custom DBpedia *Construct Validation*.

Dataset	Version	Triples	IRIs Total	Coverage	Errors	Error rate
CaliGraph [4]	2020.03.01	321,508,492	954,813,788	48.50%	30,478,073	6.58%
MusicBrainz [13]	2017.12.01	163,162,562	443,227,356	12.58%	23	0.00%
GeoNames[a]	2018.03.11	176,672,577	468,026,653	10.86%	321,865	0.63%
DBkWik [5]	2019.09.02	127,944,902	322,866,512	6.91%	18	0.00%
DNB[b]	2019.10.15	226,028,758	502,217,070	3.37%	14	0.00%

[a] https://www.geonames.org
[b] German National Library - https://www.dnb.de

encoded or incorrectly used. In the case of RDF, this demonstrates that the introduced test approach can validate links between independently produced Linked Open datasets.

Limitations. *Coverage of Construct Validation.* As demonstrated the *Construct Validation* can test for issues that are not covered by the *Syntax* or *Shape Validation*. But for fine-grained testing, to reach a 100% IRI test coverage on an extracted dataset, it is quite hard to define test cases for every used namespace and vocabulary, concerning their encoding and layouts (e.g., external links). *Comparison of releases.* The number of enabled extractors, produced artifacts, extracted languages, new tests, and mappings can change in newer releases. Therefore, it is challenging to compare evolving releases containing a different set of files and single files that provide more or fewer triples.

7   Related Work

At the conceptual level, our work is very related to the "Engineering Agile Big-Data" concepts described in [3] and inspired and based on those particular concepts. Below we discuss the related works to ours and primarily in respect to *i) data release cycle* and *ii) data quality assessment.*

Data Release Cycle. The release processes for different knowledge bases are naturally different due to the different ways of obtaining the data. Wikidata, as the most related open data release project, releases dumps on a weekly basis and publishes them in an online file directory[24] without machine-readable descriptions. In comparison, DBpedia systematically releases data artifacts accompanied with machine-readable descriptions published on the DBpedia Databus platform. This enables data consumers to develop intelligent consumer agents which can easily find and retrieve relevant data artifacts.

Besides Wikimedia, there are other open data release initiatives such as WordNet [9], BabelNet [10] and YAGO [14]. However, all these projects (with

---

[24] https://dumps.wikimedia.org/wikidatawiki/entities/.

exception Wikidata) do not provide regular *time-driven* (e.g. monthly, bi-annual or annual) releases as DBpedia does. Their current release strategy is *feature-driven* and a new data version is released as soon as a new feature or extension has been implemented. This results in delayed and irregular releases. For example, the release of YAGO 4.0 (release in March 2020) took almost three years since the previous YAGO 3.1 release (in June 2017). Similarly, BabelNet[25] performs feature-driven releases, with the latest BabelNet 4.0 release from Feb 2018 and the previous 3.7 release from Aug 2016.

Data Quality Assessment. Further, we briefly mention two projects that attempt Linked Data quality assessment by applying alternative facets.

Due to the different nature, DBpedia implements software/minidump and large-scale validation mechanism. Wikidata performs validation using the Shape Expressions Language (ShEx)[26] on top of the user generated input.

TripleCheckMate [1] describes a crowd-sourced data quality assessment approach by producing manual error reports of whether a statement conforms to a resource or can be classified as a taxonomy-based vulnerability. Their results showed a broad overview of examined errors but were tied to high efforts and offered no integration concept for further fixing procedures. On the other hand, RDFUnit is a test-driven data-debugging framework that can run automatically generated and manually generated test cases (predecessor of SHACL) against RDF datasets [7]. These automatic test cases mostly concentrate on the schema, whether domain types, range values, or datatypes adhere correctly. The results are also provided in the form of aggregated test reports.

8   Conclusion and Future Work

In this paper, we presented and combined several approaches (including *time-based*, *test-driven*, and *traceable* development principles) for increasing the agility and efficiency of knowledge extraction workflows and demonstrated it in the case of the novel DBpedia release cycle. Considering that DBpedia is an enormous open source project, we introduced a new set of extensive test methods, to offer a convenient process for community-driven feedback and development. The DBpedia Databus is used as a quality control interface, due to the utilization of traceable metadata. The *Construct Validation* test approach provides a more in-depth issue tracking checking for wrong formatted datatypes, inconsistent use of vocabularies, and the layout or encoding of IRIs produced in the extracted data. In combination with *Syntactical* and *Shape Validation*, this covers a large spectrum of possible data flaws. Moreover, it was shown that the minidump-based and large-scale test concept provides a flexible view to directly link tests with existing issues. The described workflow builds a reliable and stable base for future DBpedia (or other quality-assured data) releases. However, we presented only a few specific examples of how testing and development of the release process is improved. Therefore, the full potential of how the testing methodologies

---

[25] https://babelnet.org/stats.
[26] https://shex.io.

increase agility and productivity can only be measured after their adoption by the community in the next years. As an overall result, the new DBpedia release cycle produces over 21 billion triples per month with minimal publishing effort. As future work, we will link all created evaluation reports to Databus artifacts, similar to the explained code references (cf. Subsect. 4.2). Further, we plan to extend the usability of the release dashboard.

Acknowledgments. This work was partially supported by grants from the Federal Ministry for Economic Affairs and Energy of Germany (BMWi) for the LOD-GEOSS Project (03EI1005E) and the PLASS (01MD19003D) projects. We thank Sören Auer and the German National Library of Science and Technology (TIB) for providing servers to run the DBpedia knowledge extractions.

References

1. Acosta, M., Zaveri, A., Simperl, E., Kontokostas, D., Auer, S., Lehmann, J.: Crowdsourcing linked data quality assessment. In: Alani, H., et al. (eds.) ISWC 2013. LNCS, vol. 8219, pp. 260–276. Springer, Heidelberg (2013). https://doi.org/10.1007/978-3-642-41338-4_17
2. Beck, K., Beedle, M., van Bennekum, A., et al.: Manifesto for agile software development (2001). http://www.agilemanifesto.org/
3. Feeney, K., et al.: Engineering Agile Big-Data Systems. River Publishers Series in Software Engineering. River Publishers (2018). https://doi.org/10.13052/rp-9788770220156
4. Heist, N., Paulheim, H.: Entity extraction from Wikipedia list pages. In: Harth, A., et al. (eds.) ESWC 2020. LNCS, vol. 12123, pp. 327–342. Springer, Cham (2020). https://doi.org/10.1007/978-3-030-49461-2_19
5. Hofmann, A., Perchani, S., Portisch, J., et al.: Dbkwik: towards knowledge graph creation from thousands of wikis. In: International Semantic Web Conference (Posters, Demos & Industry Tracks) (2017). http://ceur-ws.org/Vol-1963/
6. Ismayilov, A., Kontokostas, D., Auer, S., Lehmann, J., Hellmann, S., et al.: Wikidata through the eyes of dbpedia. Semant. Web 9(4), 493–503 (2018)
7. Kontokostas, D., et al.: Test-driven evaluation of linked data quality. In: WWW (2014)
8. Lehmann, J., Isele, R., Jakob, M., Jentzsch, A., et al.: DBpedia - a large-scale, multilingual knowledge base extracted from wikipedia. SWJ 6(2) (2015)
9. Miller, G.A.: WordNet: An Electronic Lexical Database. MIT Press (1998)
10. Navigli, R., Ponzetto, S.P.: BabelNet: the automatic construction, evaluation and application of a wide-coverage multilingual semantic network. Artif. Intell. **193**, 217–250 (2012)
11. Samuelson, P.A., Nordhaus, W.D.: Microeconomics, 17th edn. McGraw-Hill Irwin, Boston (2001)
12. E.S.S. Standard: EBNF: ISO/IEC 14977: 1996 (e). 70 (1996). http://www.cl.cam.ac.uk/mgk25/iso-14977.pdf
13. Swartz, A.: Musicbrainz: a semantic web service. IEEE Intell. Syst. **17**(1), 76–77 (2002). https://doi.org/10.1109/5254.988466
14. Pellissier Tanon, T., Weikum, G., Suchanek, F.: YAGO 4: a reasonable knowledge base. In: Harth, A., et al. (eds.) ESWC 2020. LNCS, vol. 12123, pp. 583–596. Springer, Cham (2020). https://doi.org/10.1007/978-3-030-49461-2_34

15. Vrandečić, D., Krötzsch, M.: Wikidata: a free collaborative knowledgebase. Commun. ACM **57**(10), 78–85 (2014)
16. Zaveri, A., Rula, A., Maurino, A., Pietrobon, R., Lehmann, J., Auer, S.: Quality assessment for linked data: a survey. Semant. Web J. (2015)

DBpedia Archivo: A Web-Scale Interface for Ontology Archiving Under Consumer-Oriented Aspects

Johannes Frey(✉), Denis Streitmatter, Fabian Götz, Sebastian Hellmann,
and Natanael Arndt🆔

InfAI and Leipzig University, AKSW, Leipzig, Germany
{frey,streitmatter,hellmann,arndt}@informatik.uni-leipzig.de,
fabian.goetz@infai.org
https://infai.org/kilt/

Abstract. While thousands of ontologies exist on the web, a unified system for handling online ontologies – in particular with respect to discovery, versioning, access, quality-control, mappings – has not yet surfaced and users of ontologies struggle with many challenges. In this paper, we present an online ontology interface and augmented archive called DBpedia Archivo, that discovers, crawls, versions and archives ontologies on the DBpedia Databus. Based on this versioned crawl, different features, quality measures and, if possible, fixes are deployed to handle and stabilize the changes in the found ontologies at web-scale. A comparison to existing approaches and ontology repositories is given.

Keywords: Ontology archive · Ontology repository · Ontology crawling

1 Introduction

Phrases such as "A little semantics goes a long way"[1] or "Let a thousand ontologies blossom" [7] have shaped the landscape of ontologies on the Semantic Web. Ontologies are the common language spoken on the Semantic Web, they represent schema knowledge and provide a common point of integration and reference while the value of an ontology grows with its use. As the conceptual framework to globally interlink distributed knowledge, ontologies provide the backbone of the Semantic Web.

While thousands of ontologies exist on the web, a unified system for handling online ontologies has not yet surfaced and both publishers and users of ontologies struggle with many uncertainties and challenges. The main discussion and effort so far in the Semantic Web community is unbalanced and focused on authoring and publication of ontologies and linked data in general with serious

---

[1] http://www.cs.rpi.edu/~hendler/LittleSemanticsWeb.html.

Sebastian Hellmann—https://global.dbpedia.org/id/3eGWH.

E. Blomqvist et al. (Eds.): SEMANTiCS 2020, LNCS 12378, pp. 19–35, 2020.
https://doi.org/10.1007/978-3-030-59833-4_2

consequences. The community produced several guidelines, rules, methodologies and tooling for publishers neglecting users and clients. However, the variety increases uncertainty by offering too many choices, increases effort and complexity through the need to understand and implement several guidelines and provides no or unclear incentives or rewards to the publisher to comply with them.

As a consequence, the consumer is left to deal with the resulting heterogeneity, quality issues and failures. The majority of problems and challenges fall into the categories access and quality. We have identified several *Usage Challenges* which we enumerate in parentheses for reference in the remainder of the paper. Major *physical* access problems are caused by link rot (UC1) and incorrect Linked Data deployments (UC2), but most crucially there is no established, stable citation or dependency system for ontologies like Maven or DOI (UC3) - ontologies or parts of it can change or disappear anytime. Additionally, heterogeneity increases the complexity to access ontologies. There can be no, unclear or inconsistent versioning (UC4a), the versioning nomenclature can substantially vary (UC4b) and guarantees w.r.t. backward-compatibility usually remain unclear (UC4c). Various formats to serialize OWL ontologies exist (e.g. OWL-XML, RDF-XML, Manchester Syntax, Turtle; UC5). In case that an application/consumer succeeded to retrieve an ontology (version) several quality problems can prevent proper processing/usage. Parsing of the RDF snapshot can fail (UC6), problems w.r.t. licensing can prevent the usage at all (UC7) due to missing, unclear, heterogeneous (several properties and license IDs) or too restrictive or improper licensing. Finally, the fitness for use can be limited due to low quality metadata (e.g. missing labels, title; UC8) or logical inconsistencies (UC9).

In this paper, we present a web-scale ontology interface called DBpedia Archivo (acronym for ontology archive), that discovers, crawls and versions ontologies and archives as well as augments them on the DBpedia Databus [5]. The primary purpose of this interface is to help users/consumers to discover, access and validate/assess the quality/usability of ontologies in a unified way, while reducing the challenges and effort to spot and deal with the mentioned issues, such that they can focus on building stable and reliable applications. Nevertheless, we also aim to support both the consumer and the publisher by augmenting the ontology (e.g. reporting quality metrics, generating documentation). We envision in the mid/long-term, that with the help of Archivo we foster the adherence to standards (publicly showing issues, basic quality control for access to Archivo) and strengthening incentives for publishers (bad metadata e.g. no dct:title, dct:description results in worse findability and presentation in Archivo), such that the overall quality of the ontologies in the Web of Data emerges, which in return would benefit users and applications.

We argue, that a crucial factor for the success of the web were working web browsers and search engines that increased user numbers and views and created incentives to publish correct and high quality websites. Following this line, as a novel paradigm, DBpedia Archivo (see Fig. 1) proposes a consumer/application-oriented approach to the Semantic Web.

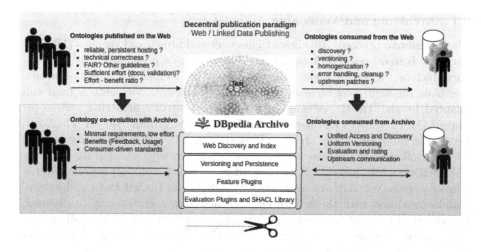

Fig. 1. Interface and platform model of Archivo

At a glance, with DBpedia Archivo we make the following **contributions**:

1. Discovery (including user suggestions), crawling, versioning, archiving and evaluation of ontologies with a high degree of **homogenization and automation**,
2. unified, stable, referenceable **identifiers for each ontology version**, so that ontology consumption becomes stable and applications, experiments and research with a specific version of an ontology, can be reproduced at any time,
3. unified time-based and Semantic Versioning enabling **auto update applications** with custom trade-off between latest changes and stability (user controlled up-to-dateness),
4. the augmented archive includes add-ins and extensions which enhance the use of an ontology, among others, generated documentation, **quality reporting** with a consumer-oriented star rating and results of validation and test steps.

In the following section we provide an overview on related work. In the subsequent section we briefly introduce the conceptual ideas of Archivo and its platform model. Sect. 4 describes the implementation. In Sect. 5 we introduce an automatically verifyable consumer rating. An evaluation of an initial crawl of ontologies based on our rating as well as a comparison of Archivo to existing ontology repositories is given in Sect. 6.

2   Related Work

Related work can be separated into three areas: archiving and versioning tools for ontologies, ontology repositories (which are compared in depth to Archivo in Sect. 6) and ontology validation and testing tools.

2.1 Archiving and Versioning

The **Memento** protocol [19] allows to discover and browse old versions (Mementos) of web resources. The Internet Archive provides a prominent service, WaybackMachine,[2] a generic archive for web resources (including a subset of ontologies from the web) accessible using Memento. Moreover, Memento is used and adapted by the **TailR** system [11], a self-deploy/service archiving system for Linked Data resources and the **Triple Pattern Fragment Server** which can be used to serve and query archived Linked Data [21] with lower infrastructural efforts. Unfortunately, Memento is currently not (widely) adopted for ontology publication and to the best of our knowledge, there is no support for Memento in ontology tools, yet. Archivo offers with SPARQL and Linked Data well-known, standardized and with the help of DataID metadata a unified way to discover, access but also query (relevant) versions of an ontology but additionally serves as a central point to discover (archived) ontologies. Realization of Memento on top of Archivo is possible and subject to future work.

SemVersion [22] proposes a methodology and Java API for RDF (and ontology) versioning inspired by CVS. It offers a structural and a form of semantic diff between two versions, achieved by performing structural diffs on semantic closures (RDF(S) entailment). The semantic diff of Archivo based on (OWL) axiom diffs goes a step further. **Quit** [2] implements an RDF versioning and collaboration system on top of Git. It provides unified access via SPARQL 1.1 on each version of an ontology and the versioning history. Both systems focus on ontology development rather than the consumer perspective.

D2V is a tool to manage and visualize user-defined changes in RDF data. In [17] it is demonstrated for ontology evolution measuring specific types of changes (e.g. added properties / labels or deprecated classes). While D2V allows very flexible, use-case/dataset specific-analysis of changes, Archivo's additional Semantic Versioning aims at making the trade-off between unified and flexible/fine-grained change reports with 3 types of changes (major, minor, patch).

Vocol [6] is an integrated environment based on Git and several services to enable collaborative vocabulary development. The workflow consists of 3 activities: modeling, population and testing (syntactic and semantic validation, competency questions), deployment of ontologies (machine- and human-readable). While some of the features (semantic diff and validation, documentation generation, custom tests for ontologies) are similar to Archivo, Vocol was designed for publishers, consumers depend on them to take advantage of the system.

2.2 Ontology Repositories and Platforms

There have been ample efforts to provide a platform, repository, library or other web services to deal with storage, search, retrieval of ontologies, some of which do not exist or work properly anymore. For reasons of brevity, we only mention approaches which are, to the best of our knowledge, still active and functional. We refer the reader to [4] for a time travel to a decade ago.

---

[2] https://archive.org/web/.

In our scope we identify 4 major characteristics of such systems. An archive persists ontologies (and its versions). A catalog associates a list of ontologies with thorough metadata. As index we denote a system that allows to search components (e.g. classes) of ontologies. A development platform is a workspace with integrated tools to create and handle ontologies.

OntoMaven [13] is a distributed ontology archiving approach based on the maven philosophy. Ontologies and its dependencies are organized in mvn artifacts. As a consequence transitive imports can be resolved and downloaded locally. A set of mvn plugins supports several aspects of ontology development lifecycles, e.g. import, creation of documentation and reports, consistency tests and versioning. Although we were not able to find any announced public repository, the ontology organization structure is very similar to the one of DBpedia Databus [5] Archivo is based on.

OBOFoundry [18] is an ontology developer initiative in the biological and biomedical domain which manually curates a catalog of approved ontologies. The registering of new ontologies follows a set of design principles (e.g. naming convention, versioning strategy) which are verified semi-automatically. The foundry operates its own PURL service to offer stable identifiers.

BioPortal [23] is another prominent catalog in the biomedical domain. It offers storage for ontology submissions and archiving to registered users and performs indexing on the latest submission. Moreover, it offers developer platform features such as user access rights and mappings between ontologies.

Linked Open Vocabularies [20] (**LOV**) is a semi-automatically curated catalog of vocabularies. It offers a search index on the terms defined in the vocabularies, a SPARQL Query endpoint and provides persistent access to the history of vocabularies. New vocabularies are discovered by analyzing (re)use of terms from archived ontologies or can be suggested by users.

Ontobee [12] creates an index for OBOFoundry and a portion of other ontologies. It serves the ontologies as linked data and provides search and browsing interfaces. Another index in the biomedical domain is the **Ontology Lookup Service** [10].

OntoHub [3] is an open ontology repository engine with versioning based on Git following Open Ontology Repository Initiative (OOR) requirements. It offers homogeneous formal representation of ontology axioms using DOL, testing with HETS and competency questions. An instance of it operates ontohub.org which is free to users and contains a plethora of ontologies, including imports from other repositories.

2.3   Ontology Evaluation and Validation

The list of literature with rules and guidelines to follow is extensive. We would like to list [9,15,24], the LD principles,[3] LOD Cloud,[4] LOV[5] and refer to their

---

[3] https://www.w3.org/DesignIssues/LinkedData.html.

[4] https://lod-cloud.net/.

[5] https://lov.linkeddata.es/Recommendations_Vocabulary_Design.pdf.

references for brevity. We picked the prominent **Ontology Pitfall Scanner! (OoPS!)** [16], also used by Archivo, as a representative for the many existing validation & evaluation approaches as it provides an excellent overview of other literature. **OnToology** [1] is a service (based on OOPS and other tools) to create pull request for ontologies hosted on GitHub to deliver test reports and documentation. It is similar to the ontology augmentation concept of Archivo, however needs to be configured and managed by the repository owner/publisher.

ROBOT [8] deserves a special mention as a highly automatized and configurable evaluator. The idea here is that sub-communities for certain domains (e.g. biological and -medical) configure and deploy the tool for their community. While similar (configure local needs, deploy local), Archivo follows a more generic approach (configure local needs, deploy global).

3 Archivo Platform Model

3.1 Versioning and Persistence on the Databus

DBpedia Archivo is built on top of the DBpedia Databus [5], which is inspired by Maven Central Repository. It uses the maven concepts publisher/group/artifact/version and ports them to a Linked Data platform, in order to manage data pipelines and enable automatic publishing and consumption of data.

Archivo is a dedicated publishing agent on the Databus.[6] Similar to [13] artifact IDs (represented as IRIs) are used as stable identifiers to reference an ontology with no regard to its evolution (UC1 and UC3). A version string appended to the artifact IRI forms a stable ID to resolve a particular version. An extension of the DataID metadata vocabulary for artifact, version, and files allows for flexible and fine-grained access using SPARQL. The concepts of time-based (UC4a/b) and semantic versioning (UC4c) support increased stability of applications while allowing automatic updates to some (user-configurable) degree.

Databus file identifiers form a stable abstraction layer independent of hosting and similar to PURL by using `dcat:downloadURL` links in the metadata. Crawled ontologies and metadata are persisted on the DBpedia download server[7]. Creating a mirrored archive of ontology versions such as Archivo is, of course, not infallible. We consider it, however, a sufficiently reliable fall-back to improve persistence of ontologies on the Semantic Web.

3.2 Evaluation Plugins and SHACL Library

DBpedia Archivo largely builds on the W3C SHACL[8] standard. While minimal basic validation as described in Sect. 5 is fixed (part SHACL, part code), the remaining validation is done via a SHACL library that is partitioned into SHACL

---

[6] https://databus.dbpedia.org/ontologies.

[7] 13 years in existence, backed up by libraries (TIB) and universities (Mannheim) who are DBpedia Association members.

[8] https://www.w3.org/TR/shacl/.

test suites for specific purposes: 1) they can encode general validation rules (e.g. from OOPS and tackle UC7), 2) they can capture specific requirements needed by Archivo features such as the automatic HTML documentation generation of LODE (UC8) (cf. next section), 3) they can be sub-community or use case-specific down to individual user projects. While at the time of writing few SHACL test suites exist, we allow online contribution and extension (Validation as a Platform) for Archivo to run in the hope to give consumers a central place to encode their requirements and also discuss and agree on more universal ones.

3.3 Feature Plugins

Feature plugins in DBpedia Archivo augment a certain aspect of the ontology, e.g. generate documentation, visualization or automatic mappings. While a complete overview is out of scope of this paper, we integrated the Live OWL Documentation Environment (LODE) [14] into Archivo, which generates a uniform HTML documentation for each version of all archived ontologies. Adding more features is straightforward. Pre-generated results make them universally available for all ontologies and absolve publishers and consumers to find, learn and deploy such ontology tools.

4   Archivo Implementation

The guiding principle for Archivo's implementation follows Jon Postel's law: "Be conservative in what you do, be liberal in what you accept from others". Being "liberal" in the context of Archivo has clear limits. While we accept ontologies in different formats, work around small mistakes (e.g. also recognizing incorrect dc:license triples instead of dct:license) (UC8) and even use recovering parsers that can skip syntax errors (UC6), we decided to be strict in all aspects that directly contradict the automatic processing of ontologies and therefore either heavily impact their usefulness or require meticulous archaeological excavation work to use and archive them. Since we invested the time to implement the most common retrieval and processing methods, our guideline is **"If DBpedia Archivo can not process it in an automatic and deterministic manner, it is likely infeasible to be processed"** based on the assumption that the Semantic Web was created for machines. One prominent example here is the missing license declaration in the FOAF RDF/XML document,[9]. While the HTML documentation includes the license using RDFa,[10] it only yielded 348 triples, compared to 631 in RDF/XML. While staying "liberal", there is no optimal automatic choice on what to accept: half the ontology with license, full ontology without license. Our strategy is that we are liberal at the launch of Archivo to allow old/unmaintained (but potentially already widely used) ontology versions to be archived but we will become more restrictive (no archiving of

---

[9] http://xmlns.com/foaf/spec/ Supplement: https://github.com/dbpedia/Archivo/tree/master/paper-supplement.

[10] The subject of the license statement is the HTML document.

new ontology (versions) that do not fulfill baseline criteria) after an establishing phase. The strictness in such cases stems from the rationale that these non-automatic and non-deterministic ontologies will eventually **cause an immeasurable and unacceptable amount of effort in the downstream network of consumers**.

4.1 Ontology Discovery and Indexing

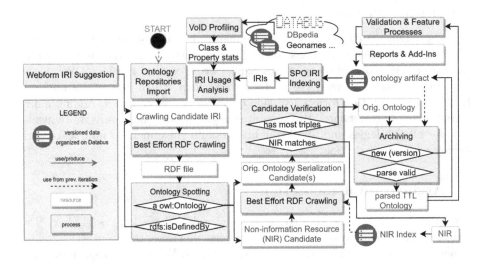

Fig. 2. Overview of iterative ontology discovery and archiving

The goal of the discovery and indexing phase is to create a distinct set (index) of non-information URIs/resource (NIR) of ontologies for each iteration as input for further crawling and processing. We devised four generic approaches to feed Archivo with ontology candidates (crawling candidate IRIs) and implemented them as a proof-of-concept.

Ontology Repositories: One straightforward way of retrieving ontology URIs is by querying already existing ontology repositories. The repository with the broadest collection of very popular ontologies of the Linked Open Data Cloud is Linked Open Vocabularies (LOV) [20], which we used in this paper. LOV provides a simple API which contains (among other metadata) candidates for non-information URIs.

Vocabulary Usage Analysis via VoID: Another approach to discover ontology candidates is by analyzing vocabulary usage in the data. Our goal here is in particular to cover all vocabularies used by datasets uploaded onto the Databus, which already contains several datasets besides DBpedia, such as Geonames, Caligraph, MusicBrainz and the German National Library, just to name a few.

As the Databus provides a controlled and harmonized environment, we generate a virtual class-based and property-based partition[11] for all RDF files on the bus, thus retrieving a list of all classes and properties.

Discovery via Links to External Ontologies: As Archivo already creates a controlled and harmonized ontology archive, we can exploit the refined collection of ontologies from the previous iteration to discover further ontology candidates. For this purpose, we extract a list of all subject, predicate and object IRIs from the ontologies itself to create more leads to properties/classes/ontology files.

Manual Suggestion: Automatic discovery is able to capture and persist most of the currently available ontologies in a forward-progressing manner. In addition manual/external suggestions of ontology candidate IRIs are accepted via web form[12] to increase Archivo's coverage and to offer an on-demand archiving function (UC3). Moreover, we consider this feature helpful for ontology engineers to test and receive feedback already during the development phase.

Subsequent to the aforementioned discovery steps we crawl/check every candidate IRI. The best effort crawling tries to download multiple RDF files via different HTTP-accept headers (in case a *robots.txt* is not disallowing access for the Archivo crawler) (UC2 and UC5). At the time of writing two additional rules are in place for considering an ontology/vocabulary as valid candidate for inclusion into Archivo: 1) the NIR needs to resolve to an RDF document rapper can read, 2) we require the existence of an entity identified by the NIR which is typed as `owl:Ontology` or `skos:ConceptScheme` (which should carry additional metadata and makes the ontology spottable in reliable way) in the triples output of the failure-tolerant parser. If multiple valid serialization candidates exist, we give preference to the serialization having the highest triple count (this will archive the correct FOAF version without license). Finally, the NIR is appended to the index and the chosen serialization is passed over for a release on the Databus. If the spotted NIR doesn't match with the candidate IRI it started with, the retrieved NIR becomes a new NIR and the process starts again (see Fig. 2). The crawling candidate IRIs representing properties and classes with a slash URI scheme require a special treatment in case the resolution does not return the ontology itself. We use `skos:inScheme` and `rdfs:isDefinedBy` as pointers to a new candidate IRI.

4.2   Analysis, Plugins and Release

Analysis and Integration of Feature Plugins: In every new snapshot, we augment the original ontology file with a parsed `ntriples`, `turtle` and `owl` version to simplify the access (UC5 and UC6). Additionally, to the plugins and validation methods described in Sect. 3, the reasoner Pellet[13] is used for checking the consistency (UC9) of the ontology and determining the OWL profile. Furthermore an OOPS report (UC8) is generated to detect common pitfalls of the

---

[11] cf. Sect. 4.5 of VoID: https://www.w3.org/TR/void/#class-property-partitions.

[12] http://archivo.dbpedia.org/add.

[13] https://github.com/stardog-union/pellet.

ontology. All reports are stored alongside the original snapshot with appropriate DataID metadata to augment the snapshot.

Release on the Databus: To deploy an ontology on the Databus we use its non-information URI as the basis for the Databus identification. The host information of the ontology's URI serves as the `groupId` and the path serves as the name for the `artifactId`. Archivo's lookup component[14] with Linked Data interface allows to resolve the mapping from a non-information URI to the stable and persistent Databus identifier.

4.3 Versioning and Persistence

Time-Based Snapshots: For all verified non-information URIs in the index, Archivo looks for new versions a few times each day. To reduce the amount of transferred data, Archivo uses the HTTP-headers `E-Tag`, `Last-Modified` and `content-length` to detect via a HEAD-request if the respective ontology resource could have changed. If any of the headers changed (or if none of the headers is available), the vocabulary is downloaded and checked locally for changes.

The local diff is performed by converting the downloaded source with rapper[15] to canonical N-Triples, sorting them and comparing them with comm[16] to determine if any triple was added or deleted. This process requires the new version to be parseable without errors. In case a change could be verified the new snapshot is released with using the fetch timestamp as version label.

Semantic Versioning: If a change in the set of triples was detected, a set of (description) logic axioms is generated for both the old and new version of the ontology and those axioms are compared to each other. In case of no changes in the axioms, no structural ontology change was done (e.g. added only labels, or ontology metadata) the change is classified as `patch`. If only new axioms were added, we consider this as a new `minor` version. If new classes/properties are added, this usually leads to no backward-compatibility problems for existing applications, but there are cases (e.g. adding a deprecated or disjoint relation to a class) which might have consequences in combination with A-boxes. Any deletion of already existing axioms (thus including renaming) is considered as `major` change potentially seriously affecting backward-compatibility. This semantic versioning "overlay" allows a more fine-grained update decision than the binary "take it or leave it" (UC4a-c). Users can refine the trade-off with custom solutions based on the semantic versioning and axiom diffs. We plan that more sophisticated versioning overlays can augment the Archivo snapshots with open contributions via Databus mods (see Sect. 7).

---

[14] http://archivo.dbpedia.org/info?o=.

[15] http://librdf.org/raptor/rapper.html.

[16] https://linux.die.net/man/1/comm.

5   A Consumer-Oriented Ontology Star Rating

Following the argumentation of Sect. 4 our proposed rating system is "liberal" to a certain degree of heterogeneity, but strict in the sense that it awards low ratings to ontologies that defy automatic or deterministic processing. The proposed star rating differs from written rules and guidelines in human language in these aspects: 1) stars are formalized and algorithmically verifiable and can be tested, 2) they are executed over the known, ontological part of the Semantic Web captured in Archivo and are meant to be delivered to consumers to quickly assess the technical usability and soundness 3) they are centrally available, frequently executed, debatable and extendable. They allow capturing and crowd-sourcing of consumer needs. We included short references to other approaches from [16][17] (integrated, see below), [8][18] and [9] (VocUse, partly applicable). From DBpedia Archivo perspective, some requirements become redundant such as the HTML documentation, which can be generated, if the appropriate SHACL test is successful. Others become more strict (machine readability).

5.1   Two Star Baseline

We consider the two star baseline as a minimal requirement for considering the ontology as a legit participant in the Semantic Web. An ontology which does not fulfill the baseline can't earn any further stars.

⋆ **Retrieval and Parsing**: All of the following criteria have to be fulfilled: (1) The non-information URI resolves to a machine readable format or a machine readable version is deterministically discoverable by other common means, (2) download was successful, (3) uses a common format implemented by Archivo, (4) at least one format was found that parses with no or few (negligible) syntactical warnings (UC6). [OBO fp2, OOPS! P37, VocUse 2]

⋆ **License I**[19]: A proper ontology declaration was found using a `owl:Ontology` and some form of license could be detected. A high degree of heterogeneity is permissible for this star regarding the used property/subproperty as well as object: license URI (resolvable linked data or web link), `xsd:string` or `xsd:anyURI` (UC7). [OBO fp1, OOPS! P38 P41, VocUse 4]

5.2   Quality Stars

On top of the two star baseline, Archivo implements additional criteria. The main rationale behind these stars is to ease effort for client implementations by homogenizing the retrieved data and the technical expectations a client can have towards mirrored ontologies by Archivo.

---

[17] http://oops.linkeddata.es/catalogue.jsp.

[18] OBO, http://obofoundry.org/principles/fp-000-summary.html, link to automated checks.

[19] SHACL test https://github.com/dbpedia/Archivo/blob/master/shacl-library/license-I.ttl.

* **License II**: We require a homogenized license declaration using `dct:license` as object property with a URI (not string or anyURI). If a resolvable Linked Data URI is used, we expect the URI to match the URI used in the machine readable license (UC7). We discovered many irregularities such as trailing '/' which violate RDF requirements that URIs need to be exactly the same in RDF as opposed to Linked Data resolution. In the future, we plan to tighten up this criterion and expect machine readable license, which we will collect on the DBpedia Databus in a similar manner as Archivo. [OBO fp1, OOPS! P41, VocUse 4]
* **Logical Fitness**: Although logical requirements such as consistency are theoretically well-defined, from a consumer perspective this star is highly implementation-specific. We measure the compatibility with currently available reasoners such as Pellet/Stardog (more to follow) and run available tasks such as consistency checks (UC9), classification, etc. since `owl:disjointWith` axioms are nice, unless they render the ontology unusable for reasoning.

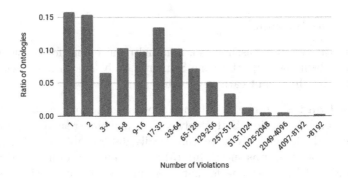

Fig. 3. Distribution of violations per ontology using SHACL-based LODE tests

Table 1. Results for Archivo (July 2020) testing and rating

#Ont.	Stars[1]	License-I[2]	License-II[2]	Consistency[2]	LODE[3]	Expressivity[4]
735	11/453/10/134/127	275/460/0	137/598/0	687/23/25	1/30/702/2	103/91/9/29/15/488

[1] Format: 0/1/2/3/4 Stars [2] Format: True/False/Error [3] Format: OK/Warnings/Violations/Error
[4] Format: OWL2 FULL/DL/QL/EL/RL/Tool Error

5.3 Further Stars and Ratings

We practiced a large amount of self-discipline not to encode more stars with our ideas and opinions as they didn't pass our own relevancy criteria (Who needs this?). Further stars and ratings could provide direct incentives for ontology publishers such as the ability to generate HTML documentation with LODE (tested with SHACL) or represent user needs, or could be of analytical nature, such as adoption and re-usage (inbound links from other ontologies and data, [9] VocUse 3 and 5).

6   Evaluation

6.1   Archivo and Rating Statistics

DBpedia Archivo consists of 735 ontologies in July 2020. The biggest fraction of it (401) was discovered via the LOV-API, 268 were discovered from prefix.cc and the rest was retrieved from the subjects, predicates and objects of the ontologies in Archivo itself (60) and user suggestions (6). Unfortunately the Usage Analysis via VOID didn't yield any new ontologies, but this feature was added at last, so the index already contained the used ontologies of datasets from the Databus. Figure 3 shows the ratio of ontologies that share a class of violations numbers. The diagram shows that, even though a small amount of ontologies are quite badly curated, the biggest share of ontologies has quite low error numbers, allowing a smooth generation of LODE documentation. Table 1 shows that more than 60% of the ontologies have less than two stars. Almost every one star rating is caused by a missing license. Since an open license is a fundamental requirement of open data, it is a bad sign for the usability of the available ontologies on the web. With more than 90% of logical consistency the ontologies are sitting pretty, but as mentioned this value can be highly implementation specific.

6.2   System Comparison

We identified 7 other (ontology repository) systems which are either very similar on a conceptual or technical level (e.g. LOV, OntoMaven) or are active systems which serve a notable set of ontologies to users. While the type and primary usage of the systems vary, we assessed them under a common set of features along the 4 dimensions coverage, recency, access and quality (see Table 2). While access and quality dimensions stem from the problem analysis, a sound strategy for both a high coverage and recency w.r.t. archived ontologies seem natural requirements from the perspective of users and tools demanding for one unified solution to efficiently tackle the problems. We argue that such a system needs to offer and be built on a high level of automation and homogenization (unified and standardized/well known practices) to successfully tackle web-scale dimensions and (if done correctly) optimize client side processes (decreased consumer side effort and increased usage benefits). We selected features reflecting this.

Archivo is the only system offering a fully automatically processed and invokable user inclusion request for an ontology (LOV requires a thorough review by its community). Apart from LOV, which analyzes referenced ontologies, none of the systems implemented a strategy to discover and include further ontologies or even use multi-layered approaches like Archivo. Besides OBO foundry and OntoMaven relying on a push-only approach, all systems use an automatic fetc.h (update) mechanism to serve the latest version of an ontology. Archivo is the only system providing Semantic Versioning and guaranteeing fully automatic unified versioning, whereas Bioportal and LOV try to extract unified timestamp versioning metadata but also partially rely on correct user input, OBO f. has a publishing principle for unified versioning, which is aut. verified but seems not

Table 2. System (feature) comparison along the dimensions coverage, r(ecentness), access and (q)uality.

Dimension		Coverage			r	Access						q
System name	TY	DO	IM	DI	UP	UV	SV	ID	PE	OF	MA	TE
Archivo	A	I	●/-	●	●	●	●	●	●	●	o/●	●
Bioportal	all	S	-/●[1]	-	●[2]	o	-	o[1]	●	-	●/●	-
LOV	C,A,I	I	o/-	o	●	o	-	o	●	●	●/●	-
OBO foundry	C	S	-/-	-	-	o	-	●	-	●	-/-	●
Ontobee	I	S	-/-	-	●	-	-	-	-	●	-/●	-
Ontohub.org	D	I	-/●[1]	-	o[3]	-	-	o	●	o	●[4]/-	●
OntoMaven repo	A	-	-/●[1]	-	-	-	-	●	●	●	o[5]/-	●
Ont. Lookup Svc	I	S	-/-	-	●	-	-	-	-	●[6]	●/●	-

Dash represents *no*, white/black filled circle represent *partial/full* support; **TY**: system type - (A)rchive, (C)atalog, (I)ndex, (D)evelopment Platform; **DO**: ont. domain focus - (S)pecialized vs. (I)ndependent; **IM**: ont. import - fully automatized user *inclusion requests/file submissions* of new ontologies; **DI**: aut. ont. discovery; **UP**: aut. update of ont.; **UV**: unified ont. versioning labels; **SV**: aut. semantic versioning of ont.; **ID**: stable ont. (version) id (IRI); **PE**: persistent ont. version access for id; **OF**: access to ont. in one unified format; **MA**: system ont. metadata access - *REST API/SPARQL*; **TE**: flexible aut. testing of ont. consistency and conformity.
[1]account/login required; [2]per ontology setting; [3]imported repos not in sync anymore; [4]reported, not accessible; [5]depending on used mvn repository systems; [6]not working due to missing void file

enforced (review revealed non-uniform versioning labels). With regard to ontology citation or dependency management of ontologies, Archivo and OntoMaven (we were not able to find any hosted ontology though) qualify by providing unified and stable, abstract identifiers (independent of the archiving system and ontology serialization) for ontologies and its version, while taking extra effort to achieve persistent access to the ontology for these identifiers. Besides Bioportal all systems try to reduce the variety of ontologies by supplying every ontology in at least one unified format. Versioning/ontology system metadata access for Archivo is designed to work via RDF and SPARQL, at the time of writing there is only a very basic REST API (and Linked Data interface) available. Both OBO f. and Archivo leverage a continuous, flexible/customizable testing system which is coordinated and performed at a central place to report issues and improve quality, in contrast to Ontohub and OntoMaven focussing on custom tests from/for publishers.

The comparison clearly shows that Archivo addresses a gap and is, to the best of our knowledge, the only system which tries to tackle the (most) user challenges at web-scale and a consumer can rely on that the archived ontology retrieved by a timestamp version resolves to the one that had been served by the ontology authority/domain at that time (no uploader hijacking and curator errors possible).

7 Future Work

On a conceptual level, we would like to develop Databus mods[20] further in order to allow users to augment the archived ontologies with modular contributions (e.g. labels for another language, mappings, another validation report, custom star ratings, etc.). This could strengthen the idea of a platform economy - users contribute what they are in need of for other users. From a technical perspective we plan to implement the Memento protocol for the Databus/Archivo and offer ontology publishers to use Archivo as "plug and play Memento as a service" for their ontologies, to support adoption of Memento and to not take away URI ownership and traffic from the publishers. We also plan to integrate more existing ontology repositories to increase the coverage for other domains. We aim to further enhance existing Databus tools, such that they improve support for special aspects of ontology consumption (e.g. automatic client side conversion of ontology formats and ontology import dependency rewriting with Databus client).

Acknowledgments. This work was partially supported by grants from the Federal Ministry for Economic Affairs and Energy of Germany (BMWi) for the LOD-GEOSS Project (03EI1005E), as well as for the PLASS Project (01MD19003D).

References

1. Alobaid, A., Garijo, D., Poveda-Villalón, M., Santana-Pérez, I., FernándezIzquierdo, A., Corcho, Ó.: Automating ontology engineering support activities with OnTool-ogy. J. Web Semant. **57** (2019)
2. Arndt, N., Naumann, P., Radtke, N., Martin, M., Marx, E.: Decentralized collab-orative knowledge management using Git. J. Web Semant. **54**, 29–47 (2019)
3. Codescu, M., Kuksa, E., Kutz, O., Mossakowski, T., Neuhaus, F.: Ontohub: a semantic repository engine for heterogeneous ontologies. Appl. Ontol. **12**(3–4), 275–298 (2017)
4. d'Aquin, M., Noy, N.F.: Where to publish and find ontologies? A survey of ontology libraries. J. Web Semant. **11**, 96–111 (2012)
5. Frey, J., Hofer, M., Obraczka, D., Lehmann, J., Hellmann, S.: DBpedia flexifusion the best of wikipedia > Wikidata > your data. In: Ghidini, C., et al. (eds.) ISWC 2019. LNCS, vol. 11779, pp. 96–112. Springer, Cham (2019). https://doi.org/10.1007/978-3-030-30796-7_7
6. Halilaj, L., et al.: VoCol: an integrated environment to support version-controlled vocabulary development. In: Blomqvist, E., Ciancarini, P., Poggi, F., Vitali, F. (eds.) EKAW 2016. LNCS (LNAI), vol. 10024, pp. 303–319. Springer, Cham (2016). https://doi.org/10.1007/978-3-319-49004-5_20
7. van Harmelen, F.: Semantic web research anno 2006: main streams, popular fal-lacies, current status and future challenges. In: Klusch, M., Rovatsos, M., Payne, T.R. (eds.) CIA 2006. LNCS (LNAI), vol. 4149, pp. 1–7. Springer, Heidelberg (2006). https://doi.org/10.1007/11839354_1

---

[20] http://dev.dbpedia.org/Databus_Mods.

8. Jackson, R.C., Balhoff, J.P., Douglass, E., Harris, N.L., Mungall, C.J., Overton, J.A.: ROBOT: a tool for automating ontology workflows. BMC Bioinform. **20**(1), 407:1–407:10 (2019)
9. Janowicz, K., Hitzler, P., Adams, B., Kolas, D., Vardeman, C.: Five stars of linked data vocabulary use. Semant. Web **5** (2014)
10. Jupp, S., Burdett, T., Leroy, C., Parkinson, H.E.: A new ontology lookup service at EMBL-EBI. In: SWAT4LS (2015)
11. Meinhardt, P., Knuth, M., Sack, H.: TailR: a platform for preserving history on the web of data. In: SEMANTiCS (2015)
12. Ong, E., Xiang, Z., Zhao, B., Liu, Y.: Ontobee: a linked ontology data server to support ontology term dereferencing, linkage, query and integration. Nucleic Acids Res. **45**(D1) (2016)
13. Paschke, A., Schäfermeier, R.: OntoMaven - maven-based ontology development and management of distributed ontology repositories. In: Nalepa, G.J., Baumeister, J. (eds.) Synergies Between Knowledge Engineering and Software Engineering. AISC, vol. 626, pp. 251–273. Springer, Cham (2018). https://doi.org/10.1007/978-3-319-64161-4_12
14. Peroni, S., Shotton, D., Vitali, F.: The live OWL documentation environment: a tool for the automatic generation of ontology documentation. In: Teije, A., et al. (eds.) EKAW 2012. LNCS (LNAI), vol. 7603, pp. 398–412. Springer, Heidelberg (2012). https://doi.org/10.1007/978-3-642-33876-2_35
15. Polleres, A., Kamdar, M.R., Fernández, J.D., Tudorache, T., Musen, M.A.: A more decentralized vision for Linked Data. Semantic Web **11**(1), 101–113 (2020)
16. Poveda-Villalón, M., Gómez-Pérez, A., Suárez-Figueroa, M.C.: OOPS! (OntOlogy Pitfall Scanner!): an on-line tool for ontology evaluation. IJSWIS **10**(2), 7–34 (2014)
17. Roussakis, Y., Chrysakis, I., Stefanidis, K., Flouris, G.: D2V: a tool for defining, detecting and visualizing changes on the data web. In: ISWC P&D. CEUR Workshop Proceedings (2015)
18. Smith, B., Ashburner, M., Rosse, C., Bard, J.: The OBO foundry: coordinated evolution of ontologies to support biomedical data integration. Nat. Biotechnol. **25**(11), 1251–1255 (2007)
19. de Sompel, H.V., Sanderson, R., Nelson, M.L., Balakireva, L., Shankar, H., Ainsworth, S.: An HTTP-based versioning mechanism for linked data. In: LDOW. CEUR Workshop Proceedings (2010)
20. Vandenbussche, P., Atemezing, G., Poveda-Villalón, M., Vatant, B.: Linked Open Vocabularies (LOV): a gateway to reusable semantic vocabularies on the Web. Semant. Web **8**(3), 437–452 (2017)
21. Vander Sande, M., Verborgh, R., Hochstenbach, P., Van de Sompel, H.: Toward sustainable publishing and querying of distributed Linked Data archives. J. Doc. (2018)
22. Völkel, M., Groza, T.: SemVersion: an RDF-based ontology versioning system. In: ICWI (2006)
23. Whetzel, P.L., Noy, N.F., Shah, N.H., Alexander, P.R.: BioPortal: enhanced functionality via new Web services from the NCBO to access and use ontologies in software applications. Nucleic Acids Res. **39**, 541–545 (2011)
24. Wilkinson, M.D., Dumontier, M., Aalbersberg, I.J., Appleton, G.: The FAIR Guiding Principles for scientific data management and stewardship. Sci. Data **3**, 160018 (2016)

A Knowledge Retrieval Framework for Household Objects and Actions with External Knowledge

Alexandros Vassiliades[1,2]([⊠]), Nick Bassiliades[1], Filippos Gouidis[2], and Theodore Patkos[2]

[1] Department of Computer Science, Aristotle University of Thessaloniki, Thessaloniki, Greece
{valexande,nbassili}@csd.auth.gr
[2] Institute of Computer Science, Foundation for Research and Technology, Hellas, Heraklion, Greece
{gouidis,patkos}@ics.forth.gr

Abstract. In the field of domestic cognitive robotics, it is important to have a rich representation of knowledge about how household objects are related to each other and with respect to human actions. In this paper, we present a domain dependent knowledge retrieval framework for household environments which was constructed by extracting knowledge from the VirtualHome dataset (http://virtual-home.org). The framework provides knowledge about sequences of actions on how to perform human scaled tasks in a household environment, answers queries about household objects, and performs semantic matching between entities from the web knowledge graphs DBpedia, ConceptNet, and WordNet, with the ones existing in our knowledge graph. We offer a set of predefined SPARQL templates that directly address the ontology on which our knowledge retrieval framework is built, and querying capabilities through SPARQL. We evaluated our framework via two different user evaluations.

Keywords: Ontology · Cognitive robotics · Knowledge retrieval framework · Semantic similarity

1 Introduction

Ontologies have been used in many cognitive robotic systems which perform object identification [8,22,31], affordances detection (i.e. the functionality of an object) [2,16,25], and for robotic platforms that work as caretakers for people in a household environment [20,34]. We can see an extensive survey on these topics in [9]. In this paper, we introduce a novel knowledge retrieval framework[1] for household objects and actions that can be used as part of the knowledge representation component of a cognitive robotic system, which is connected with

---

[1] https://github.com/valexande/HomeOntology.

E. Blomqvist et al. (Eds.): SEMANTiCS 2020, LNCS 12378, pp. 36–52, 2020.
https://doi.org/10.1007/978-3-030-59833-4_3

a custom made semantic matching algorithm to enrich its knowledge. Moreover, to the best of our knowledge our ontology is the largest one about objects and actions, as well as activities (i.e. set of object-action relations).

Common Sense (CS) knowledge is an aspect that is desired by any Artificial Intelligence (AI) system. Eventhough, there are no strict definitions on what we should consider CS knowledge. Our knowledge retrieval framework can help tackle queries that require CS reasoning, on how objects are related, and how we can perform a human scaled task. Some example queries are *"What actions can I perform with a pot?"*, or *"What other objects are related to knife, plate, and fork?"*, or even *"What can I turn on if I am in the living room?"*. Furthermore, our framework can recommend sequences of actions on how to perform a human scaled task, like *"How can I make a sandwich?"*. Our framework is based on a domain-specific ontology that we have developed which contains knowledge from the VirtualHome dataset [17,23]. The ontology is built in OWL [19] and the Knowledge Base (KB) can be easily extended by adding new instances of objects, actions, and activities.

Due to the fact that the VirtualHome dataset covers a restricted set of objects, in order to be able to retrieve knowledge about objects on a larger scale, we developed a mechanism that can take advantage of external open knowledge bases in order to retrieve knowledge or answer queries about objects that do not exist in our KB. To this end, we have devised a semantic match making algorithm that retrieves semantically related knowledge out of three web knowledge graphs, namely DBpedia [5], ConceptNet [18], and WordNet [30]. When our framework cannot find an entity in its own KB, it uses the knowledge existing in the aforementioned KBs, to relate the unknown entity with one in our local KB. Also, the framework can provide some general knowledge about objects such as *"How much fat does a banana have?"*, with predefined SPARQL query templates addressed to DBpedia. We notice that our framework performs semantic matching only with the aforementioned ontologies.

The knowledge retrieval framework was evaluated with two different user evaluation methods. In the first one, 42 subjects were asked on how satisfied they were with the returned answers on different query categories. The results seem promising with a 82% score. While in the other evaluation, we gathered a gold standard dataset for a set of queries that our framework can answer, from a group of 5 persons not part of the first group. Then, we asked a group of 34 people to give us answers to the same queries using only information from each dataset, and we compared these with the answers of our knowledge retrieval framework.

The rest of the paper is organized as follows. In Sect. 2, we present the related work. In Sect. 3, we describe our approach and the architecture of our knowledge retrieval framework. Next, in Sect. 4 we present the results of the user evaluation. Finally, in Sect. 5 we give a discussion and the conclusion.

2   Related Work

Our study balances between two fields. Firstly, our knowledge retrieval framework can be fused in a cognitive robotic system acting in a household environment. The cognitive robotic system will then enhance its knowledge about which objects are related, object properties, affordances understanding, and to semantically connect entities in its KB with entities in DBpedia, ConceptNet, WordNet. Secondly, if one considers only the ontology part of our work then this ontology would be close to other Linked Open Data KBs about products, and household objects. For the first case, we need to mention that our study can stand only as part of the knowledge representation component of a cognitive robotic system that can fill reasoning gaps.

Property extraction and creation methods, between objects in a household environment, have been implemented in many robotic platforms [8,22,33]. Usually an object identification is done based on the shape and the dimensions perceived by the vision module, or in some cases [2,31] reasoning mechanisms such as grasping area segmentation, or a physics based module contribute to understand an object's label. In [27], spatial-contextual knowledge is used to infer the label of an object, for example the object x is usually found near objects $y_1, \ldots, y_n$, or x is found on y. Even though these are state of the art frameworks, the robotic platform has to extract information from two or more different ontologies, in order to link an object with an affordance.

The aspect of affordances understanding based on an ontology, mainly with OWL format, is widely studied. In [16,25], authors try to understand affordances by observing human motion. They capture the semantics of a human movement, and correlate it with an action label. On the other hand, Jäger et al. [13] have connected objects with physical and functional properties, but the functional properties which can be considered as affordances, capture a very abstract concept, as they define only the properties *containment, support, movability, blockage*. Similarly, Beßler et al. [3] define 18 actions that can be performed on objects if some preconditions hold in each case, such as if the objects are reachable, the material of the object, among others. The affordances existing in our knowledge retrieval framework are more than 70, combined with other features. Thus, we can offer greater plurality from frameworks like the aforementioned ones.

Our study attempts to fill the gap found in the previous studies and develop a knowledge retrieval framework that would complete the missing knowledge. Our framework, compared to the previous ones can offer: (i) a predefined KB of objects related to actions, (ii) a KB with sequences of actions to achieve human scaled tasks, and (iii) a mechanism that uses semantic match making between an entity that does not exist in our KB with an entity in the KB.

Our semantic matching algorithm was mostly inspired by the works of Young et al. [35], and Icarte et al. [12] where they use CS knowledge from the web ontologies DBpedia, ConceptNet, and WordNet to find the label of unknown objects. As well as from the studies [6,36], where the label of the room can be understood through the objects that the cognitive robotic system perceived from its vision module. One drawback that can be noticed in these works, is that all of them depend on only one ontology. Young et al. compares only the DBpedia comment boxes between the entities, Icarte et al. acquires only the property values from ConceptNet of the entities, and [6,36] on the synonyms, hypernyms, and hyponyms of WordNet entities.

As for the second part, our study can be compared with an already existing product ontology, such as the product ontologies found in [24,32], the more recent [28], and the general purpose ontology GoodRelations [10]. Our difference is that these ontologies offer information about objects, geometrical, physical, and material properties, and create object taxonomies and hierarchical relations. Instead, we have implemented knowledge about object affordances and we represent knowledge, about objects through their affordances. Furthermore, O-Pro [4] is an ontology for object-affordance relations, but is considerably smaller with respect to the quantity of objects and affordances. Thus, to the best of our knowledge we offer the largest ontology about object affordances, in a household environment.

3   Our Approach

In this section, we describe in detail the architecture and the different aspects of our knowledge retrieval framework. In the first subsection, we describe the dataset from which we took knowledge and fused in our schema. Next, we present the ontology that is the main component of our framework. In the last subsection, we describe the algorithm that semantically matches entities from DBpedia, ConceptNet, and WordNet, with entities in our KB.

3.1   Household Dataset

The VirtualHome dataset [17,23] contains activities that people do at home. For each activity, there are different descriptions on how to perform them. The descriptions are present in the form of sequence of actions, i.e., steps that contain an action related with an object or objects, illustrated in Example 1. Moreover, the dataset offers a virtual environment representation for each sequence of actions with Unity[2]. The dataset contains ~2800 sequences of actions, for human scaled activities. Moreover, the dataset holds more than 500 objects, usually found in a household environment, which are semantically connected with each other, and with specific human scaled actions.

Example 1. Browse Internet
Comment: walk to living room. look at computer. switch on computer. sit in chair. watch computer. switch off computer.

> [Walk] ⟨living_room⟩ (1)
> [Walk] ⟨computer⟩ (1)
> [Find] ⟨computer⟩ (1)
> [TurnTo] ⟨computer⟩ (1)
> [LookAt] ⟨computer⟩ (1)
> [SwitchOn] ⟨computer⟩ (1)
> [Find] ⟨chair⟩ (2)

---

[2] https://unity.com.

[Sit] ⟨chair⟩ (2)
[Watch] ⟨computer⟩ (1)
[SwitchOff] ⟨computer⟩ (1)

Each sequence of actions has a template: (a) Activity Label, (b) Comment, i.e. small description, and (c) the sequence of actions. Each step has the general form shown in (1):

$$[Action]\langle Object_1\rangle(ID_1)\dots\langle Object_n\rangle(ID_n) \tag{1}$$

where *Action* is the human scaled action, $Object_1,\dots,Object_n$ are the objects on which the action is performed ($n \in \mathbb{N}$), and $ID_1,\dots,ID_n$ are the unique identity numbers between the objects that represent the same natural object. In our experiments we have approximately 500 objects, but due to the fact that the ontology can be freely extended with objects, we consider n as a natural number.

3.2 Ontology

The main component of our knowledge retrieval framework is the ontology that was inspired by the VirtualHome dataset. Figure 1a presents part of the ontology concepts, while Fig. 1b the relationships between the major concepts.

The class *Activity* contains some subclasses which follow the hierarchy provided by the dataset; these were hand-coded. Moreover, the instances of these classes are the sequence of actions presented in the KB of the dataset. The class *Activity* is connected through the property *listOfSteps* with the class *Step*. Additionally, the class *Step* is connected through the properties *object* and *step_type* with the classes *ObjectType* and *StepType*, respectively. Next, the class *Object-Type* contains the labels of all the objects found in the sequences. On the other hand, the class *StepType* is similar to *ObjectType* as it gives natural language labels to the steps.

We have represented every sequence of actions as a list, because this gave us stronger coherency and interaction on the knowledge provided by the activity. Thus, we can answer queries like *"What is the third step in the sequence of activity X?"*, or *"Return all the sequences where firstly I walk to the living room, then I open the TV, and after that I sit on the sofa"*, information very crucial for a system with planning capabilities. Also, we have developed an instance generator algorithm that transforms the sequences of actions from the form of Example 1 into instances of classes in our ontology. The class that the sequence belongs to, is provided by the Activity label. We give such an instance in Example 2.

Example 2.

```
:browse_internet132 rdf:type :BrowseInternet ;
    :listOfSteps (
    :walk1607 :walk1608  :find1609
    :turnto1610 :lookat1611 :switchon1612
    :find1613    :sit1614 :watch1615 :switchoff1616 ) ;
    rdfs:comment ''walk to living room...'' ; .
```

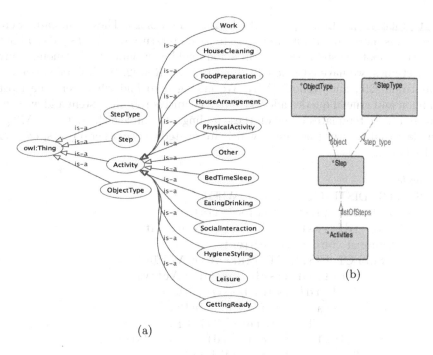

(a)

(b)

Fig. 1. (a) Part of Ontology Scheme (b) Ontology Properties.

Each step shown in the property *listOfSteps* is an instance of the class *Step*. Each step has a unique ID that distinguishes it from all the other steps. Example 3 shows an instance step from the *listOfSteps*, and Example 4 the object and action with which the instance is connected from the *ObjectType* and *StepType* classes.

Example 3.
```
:walk1608 rdf:type :Step ;
      :object :computer1 ;
      :steptype :walk .
```

Example 4.
```
:computer1 rdf:type :ObjectType;
     rdfs:label ''computer''@en.

:walk rdf:type :StepType;
     rdfs:label ''walk''@en .
```

After constructing and populating the ontology, we have developed a library in Python that constructs SPARQL queries addressed to the ontology and fetches answers. The library consists of 9 predefined query templates that represent the most probable question types to the household ontology. These templates were consider as more important after an extensive literature review of studies about cognitive robotic systems that act in a household environment [9]. Among many other studies, we have considered primarily KnowRob [2,31], RoboSherlock [1], RoboBrain [29], and RoboCSE [7]. We managed to find what were the most common and crucial queries addressed to a cognitive robotic system and we constructed these templates based on these findings. Example 5 shows the SPARQL template that returns the objects which are related to two other objects, *Object1* and *Object2*.

Example 5.
```
SELECT DISTINCT ?object WHERE{
    ?instance :listOfSteps ?list .
    ?list rdf:rest*/rdf:first ?element.
    ?element :object ?object
        SELECT DISTINCT ?instance WHERE{
            ?int1 rdfs:subClassOf :Activity .
            ?in1 rdfs:subClassOf ?int1 .
            ?instance rdf:type ?in1;
                :listOfSteps ?list1 .
            ?list1 rdf:rest*/rdf:first ?step1.
            ?step1 :object :Object1 .
            ?int2 rdfs:subClassOf :Activity .
            ?in2 rdfs:subClassOf ?int2 .
            ?instance rdf:type ?in2;
                :listOfSteps ?list2 .
            ?list2 rdf:rest*/rdf:first ?step2.
            ?step2 :object :Object2.}}}
```

Alternatively, ad-hoc SPARQL queries can be asked to the ontology, such as Example 6 were an user wants to see the objects involved in the activity, *activity1*.

Example 6.
```
SELECT DISTINCT ?object WHERE{
    :activity1 :listOfSteps ?list .
    ?list rdf:rest*/rdf:first ?step .
    ?step :object ?object}
```

Therefore, users can hand pick one of the predefined queries and then give the keywords that are needed in order to fill the SPARQL template (Example 5), or they can write their own SPARQL query to access the information they desire (Example 6).

3.3 Semantic Matching Algorithm

Due to the fact that the dataset upon which the knowledge retrieval framework was constructed has a finite number of objects, in order to be able to retrieve knowledge about objects on a larger scale, we developed a mechanism that can take advantage of the web knowledge graphs DBpedia, ConceptNet, and Word-Net to answer queries about objects that do not exist in our KB. This would broaden the range of queries that the framework can answer, and would overcome the downside of our framework being dataset oriented. Algorithm 1 was implemented using Python. The libraries *Request* and *NLTK*[3] offer web APIs for all three aforementioned ontologies. Similar methods can be found in [12,35], where they also exploit the CS knowledge existing in web ontologies. Algorithm 1 starts by getting as input any word that is part of the English language; we check this by obtaining the WordNet entity, line 3. The input is given by the user implicitly, when he gives a keyword in a query that does not exist in the KB of the framework.

Subsequently, we turn to ConceptNet, and we collect the properties and values for the input word, line 4. In our framework, we collect only the values of some properties such as *RelatedTo, UsedFor, AtLocation*, and *IsA*. We choose these properties because they are the most related to our target application of providing information for household objects. Also, we acquire the weights that ConceptNet offers for each triplet. These weights represent how strong the connection is between two different entities with respect to a property in the ConceptNet graph, and are defined by the ConceptNet community. Therefore, we end up with a hash map of the following form:

$$\left\{ Property_1 : \left[\left(entity_1^1, weight_1^1 \right), \ldots, \left(entity_m^1, weight_m^1 \right) \right], \ldots, \right.$$

$$\left. Property_l : \left[\left(entity_1^l, weight_1^l \right), \ldots, \left(entity_k^l, weight_k^l \right) \right] \right\}$$

for $m, l, k \in \mathbb{N} \backslash \{0\}$.

Then, we start extracting semantic similarity between the given entity and the returned property values using WordNet and DBpedia, lines 5–8. Firstly, we find the least common path that the given entity has with each returned value from ConceptNet, in WordNet, line 9. The knowledge in WordNet is in the form of a direct acyclic graph with hyponyms and hypernyms. Thus, in each case we obtain the number of steps that are needed to traverse from one entity to another. Subsequently, we turn to DBpedia to extract comment boxes of each entity using SPARQL, lines 11–13. If DBpedia does not return any results, we search the entity in Wikipedia, which has a better search engine, and with the returned URL we ask again DBpedia for the comment box, based on the mapping scheme between Wikipedia URLs and DBpedia URIs, lines 14–20. Notice that when we encounter a redirection list we acquire the first URL of the list which in most cases is the desired entity, and acquire the comment box.

The comment box of the input entity is compared with each comment box of the returned entities from ConceptNet, using the TF-IDF algorithm to extract semantic similarity, line 21. Here we follow a policy which prescribes that the descriptions of two objects which are semantically related will contain common

---

[3] https://www.nltk.org.

words. We preferred TF-IDF despite its limitations, as it may miss some words only from the difference of one letter, because we did not want to raise the complexity of the framework using pre-trained embedding vectors like Glove [21], Word2Vec [26], or FastText [14], this remains as future work.

Algorithm 1: Semantic Matching Algorithm

---

1 **Input:** entity
2 **Output:** hash_semantic_similarity
3 **if** *entity* **in** *WordNet* **then**
4   hash_property_values = get.ConceptNet_property_values(entity)
5   Comment_Box_Input = get.DBpediaCommentBox(entity)
6   hash_semantic_similarity = {}
7   **for** *property* **in** *hash_property_values* **do**
8   **for** *value* **in** *hash_property_values[property]* **do**
9   WordNet_Path = get.WordNetPath(entity,value)
10   Commnet_Box = ∅
11   **if** *value* **in** *DBpedia* **then**
12   Comment_Box = get.DBpediaCommentBox(value)
13   **end**
14   **if** *Comment_Box = ∅* **then**
15   wiki_entity = get.WikipediaEntityURL(value)
16   Comment_Box = get.DBpediaCommentBox(wiki_entity)
17   **end**
18   **if** *Comment_Box = ∅* **then**
19   **continue**
20   **end**
21   weight_TFIDF = TF-IDF(Commen_Box_Input,Comment_Box)
             hash_semantic_similarity[property] = (value, Similarity(entity, value))
22   **end**
23   **end**
24   hash_semantic_similarity = sorted(hash_semantic_similarity)
25 **end**

In order to define the semantic similarity between the entities, we have devised a new metric that is based on the combination of WordNet paths, TF-IDF scores, and ConceptNet weights Eq. (2). We choose this specific metric because it takes into consideration the smallest WordNet path, the ConceptNet weights, and the TF-IDF scores. TF-IDF and ConceptNet scores have a positive contribution to the semantic similarity of two words. On the other hand, the bigger the path is between two words in WordNet the smaller the semantic similarity is.

$$Sim(i,v) = \frac{1}{WNP(i,v)} + TFIDF(i,v) + CNW(i,p,v) \qquad (2)$$

In Eq. 2, i is the entity given as input by the user, and v is each one of the different values returned from ConceptNet properties. $CNW(i,p,v)$ is the weight that ConceptNet gives for the triplet (i,p,v), and p stands for the property that connects i and v. $TFIDF(i,v)$ is the score returned by the TF-IDF algorithm when comparing the DBpedia comment boxes of i and v. $WNP(i,v)$ is a two parameter function that returns the least common path between i and v, in the WordNet direct acyclic graph.

In case i and v have at least one common hypernym (ch), then we acquire the smallest path for the two words, whereas in case i and v, do not have a common hypernym (nch), we add their depths. Let $depth(\cdot)$ be the function that returns the number of steps needed to reach from the root of WordNet to a given entity, then:

$$WNP(i,v) = \begin{cases} min_{c \in C} \{depth(i) + depth(v) - 2 * depth(c)\} & \text{ch} \\ depth(i) + depth(v) & \text{nch} \end{cases} \quad (3)$$

where C is the set of common hypernyms for i and v. $WNP(\cdot, \cdot)$ will never be zero, as two different entities in a direct acyclic graph will always have at least one step path between them.

The last step of the algorithm sorts the semantic similarity results of the entities with respect to the ConceptNet property, and stores the new information into a hash map, line 24. An example of the returned information is given in Example 7 where the Top-5 entities for each property are displayed, if there exist as many.

Example 7. coffee IsA: stimulant, beverage, acquired_taste, liquid.
coffee AtLocation: sugar, mug, office, cafe.
coffee RelatedTo: cappuccino, iced_coffee, irish_coffee, turkish_coffee, plant.
coffee UsedFor: refill.

4   Evaluation

We evaluated our knowledge retrieval framework via two different user evaluations. Firstly, by asking people how much they are satisfied with the results returned. Basically, we wanted to see if the answers returned by our framework satisfied the users in terms of CS. Due to the fact that we cannot define strict rules on what can be considered as CS, each subject gives their personal opinion to evaluate how satisfied they are with each answer. Thus, we asked for a score from 1 to 5 to eight categories of queries. Each person had to evaluate 40 answers (5 queries of each of the eight categories). Subjects were presented with the Top-5 answers returned for each query. We tried to find people both related to Computer Sciences (CSc) and people not related to Computer Science (N-CSc), resulting in 19 and 23 subjects, respectively. We also made another clustering with the same people based on their education level, Workers 13 (W) that did not go to University, Bachelor/Master Students 23 (B/M), PhD Students 6 (P).

The categories of queries that were evaluated are the following: Q1: *"On what objects can I perform the actions X1,..,Xn if I am in room Y?"*, Q2: *"On what objects can I perform the actions X1,..,Xn?"*, Q3: *"What can I do with objects O1,...,Om?"*, Q4: *"What objects are related to objects O1,...,Om?"*, Q5: *"Give me the category of activities for X"*, Q6: *"Give me related objects to O1,...,Om"*, Q7: *"Give me similar action(-s) to A"*, and Q8: *"Recommend an Activity based on the description A"*. Notice that in Q4, we addressed queries with objects that do not exist in our KB, to see how satisfied people are with the recommendations from Algorithm 1. Table 1 and Table 2 present the Mean and Variance scores, respectively. The results are rounded to two decimals in all the tables.

Table 1. Table with Mean scores for Q1-Q8.

	General	W	B/M	P	CSc	N-CSc
Q1	4.20	4.18	4.17	4.22	4.21	4.29
Q2	4.35	4.36	4.39	4.32	4.39	4.35
Q3	4.08	4.08	4.16	4.06	4.10	4.08
Q4	3.73	3.72	3.70	3.74	3.72	3.73
Q5	4.19	4.16	4.24	4.16	4.16	4.18
Q6	4.11	4.09	4.12	4.10	4.11	4.09
Q7	3.99	4.09	3.97	3.95	3.91	4.06
Q8	4.12	4.10	4.16	4.25	4.02	4.09
Mean	4.10	4.1	4.11	4.10	4.08	4.10

Table 2. Table with Variance scores for Q1-Q8.

	General	W	B/M	P	CSc	N-CSc
Q1	0.96	1.52	0.95	0.78	1.20	0.74
Q2	0.80	0.83	0.76	0.92	0.71	0.87
Q3	1.12	0.5	1.44	0.91	1.25	1.06
Q4	1.52	1.06	1.52	1.69	1.51	1.51
Q5	1.61	1.54	1.59	1.65	1.73	1.49
Q6	0.98	0.86	0.95	1.09	0.97	0.98
Q7	1.75	1.75	1.82	1.38	1.88	1.66
Q8	1.56	1.46	1.54	1.74	1.64	1.52
Variance	1.20	1.13	1.21	1.21	1.26	1.13

As we can see, we obtained an overall of 4.10/5, which translates to an 82% score. Moreover, regarding the low score of Q4 in comparison to other queries we can comment the following. This happened because we had a very high threshold value to the *Ratcliff-Obershelp* string similarity metric, which compared the returned results from Algorithm 1 with the ones in our KB. On top of that, we did not display the recommendation from Algorithm 1; instead, we displayed the entity from our KB with which the result of Algorithm 1 was close enough. The threshold was 0.8 and we reduced it to 0.6; for smaller values the recommendations of Algorithm 1 in most cases were not related to our target application. Therefore, we reduced the value of the threshold and displayed the web KB recommendation. We performed these changes in order to affect only

Q4. The new results are displayed in Table 3. We observe that the Mean score for Q4 increased by 13.5%, and the Variance shows that the scoring values came closer to the Mean value by 0.89.

Table 3. Table with Mean and Variance scores for Q4, with the new changes.

	General	W	B/M	P	CSc	N-CSc
Mean	4.41	4.35	4.36	4.6	4.45	4.36
Variance	0.61	0.74	0.65	0.39	0.42	0.73

In our second evaluation, we asked from 5 subjects not part of the first group to give us their own answers in the queries Q1-Q7, apart from Q4 (we shall denote this by Q1-Q7\Q4). We omitted Q4 and Q8 because we consider them as less important for evaluating the capabilities of our knowledge retrieval framework. More specifically, from the viewpoint of a user Q4 is similar to Q6, so there was no point asking it again. On the other hand, for the Q8 the 5 subjects were reluctant to answer it because they considered it very time consuming (it required to provide 25 full sentences; not just words as in the case of the other queries), so we could not gather a quantitatively appropriate dataset. Therefore, the 5 subjects had to give us 5 answers based only on their own opinion for 5 queries from each one of Q1-Q7\Q4. We resulted with a baseline dataset of 125 answers for each query. Next, 34 subjects from the first evaluation agreed to proceed with the second round of evaluation. Each one had to give one answer, for 5 queries from each one of the queries Q1-Q7\Q4 (5 * 6 = 30 answers in total) picked from the aforementioned dataset.

$$Topi = \frac{Number\ of\ correct\ answers\ in\ first\ i\ choices}{Number\ of\ answers\ in\ users\ category\ j} \tag{4}$$

where $i = 1, 3, 5$, and $j \in \{ W,\ B/M,\ P,\ CSc,\ N\text{-}CSc \}$. Then, we compared these answers with what our knowledge retrieval framework returned to each query in the first choice (Top1), the three first choices (Top3), and in the five first choices (Top5). The results are in Table 4, and they show the precision of the system Eq. (4).

Table 4. Table with Top1–Top3–Top5 scores.

	General	W	B/M	P	CSc	N-CSc
Top1	71.1%	71.1%	72.9%	63.3	71.4%	71.0%
Top3	80.7%	71.1%	82.2%	75.8%	81.6%	80.1%
Top5	84.1%	82.7%	89.6%	83.3%	83.8%	84.3%

We see that we achieved a 71.1% score in the Top1 results returned by our knowledge retrieval framework, which is high if we take into consideration that this is not a data driven framework which could learn the connections between the queries and answers, nor use embeddings between queries and answers that could point to the correct answer, therefore we gave a margin of error. Hence, we also display the Top3 and Top5 choices, where we see significant improvement by 9.6% and 13%, respectively.

Evaluation Discussion: The evaluation unfortunately could not be done with immediate interaction with the framework, as we have not yet developed a Web API. For the first evaluation, the subjects were given spreadsheets with the queries and their answers and they had to evaluate each one of them. As for the second part, 5 subjects not part of the first group where given the queries Q1-Q7\Q4, and they had to give their own answer, from where we collected the gold standard dataset. This procedure was done again through spreadsheets. Subsequently, 34 subjects from the first evaluation were asked to answer Q1-Q7\Q4 using as options the words from the gold standard dataset. Therefore, the latter group were given the stack of potential answers for each query and a spreadsheet with the queries Q1-Q7\Q4.

Considering to potential biases we notice that between the first and second evaluation there was a time lapse of over 40 d, so we doubt that any of the subjects remembered any answer from the first evaluation. Secondly, the queries were formed after an extensive literature review of what is commonly considered as crucial knowledge for cognitive robotic systems interacting with humans in a household environment. Furthermore, although we have 9 predefined SPARQL templates we have used only 8 of them in the first evaluation; this is because the one that was omitted involves the activities that were part of the VirtualHome dataset, so we have considered that this was already evaluated by previous related work.

Finally, looking at the results of the evaluation we drive the following conclusions. Firstly, the large percentage (82%) on how much satisfied with the answers of our knowledge retrieval framework the subjects are, signifies that our framework can be used by any cognitive robotic system acting in a household environment as a primary (or secondary) source of knowledge. Secondly, the second method of evaluation implies that our knowledge retrieval framework could be used as a baseline for evaluating other cognitive robotic systems acting in a household environment. Thirdly, the scores that Algorithm 1 achieved, show that it can be used as an individual service for semantically matching entities of a knowledge graph with entities from ConceptNet, DBpedia, and WordNet as it can be easily extended with more properties.

5   Discussion and Conclusion

In this paper, we presented a knowledge retrieval framework that can be fused in a cognitive robotic system that acts in a household environment, and an ontology schema. More specifically, we extracted information from the VirtualHome dataset to fuse it into our framework. Furthermore, with an instance generator algorithm we translated the activities as instances of the ontology classes. Therefore, we obtained knowledge, about how actions and objects are related, what objects are related with each other, what objects and actions exist in an activity, and suggestions on how to perform an activity in a household environment, through a set of predefined SPARQL query templates. The knowledge retrieval framework can also address hand-coded SPARQL queries to its own KB. Additionally, we broadened the range of queries the framework can answer, by developing a Semantic Matching Algorithm that finds semantic similarity, between entities existing in our KB and entities from the knowledge graphs of DBpedia, ConceptNet, and WordNet.

The problem of building an ontology schema that contains a wide variety of instances and properties, is well studied [11,15]. The same does not hold when we try to fuse CS knowledge in an KB, therefore usually methods that acquire CS either from a local KB, or a combination of local and web KBs are used. Unfortunately, fusing CS knowledge and reasoning in an ontology is not a very well-studied area, and the methods presented until now can rarely be generalized. CS knowledge and the capability of a cognitive robotic system to answer CS related queries offers flexibility.

We consider that we made a contribution in this direction by presenting a knowledge retrieval framework that can provide knowledge to a cognitive robotic system to answer questions that require CS reasoning. Looking at the results of our two evaluations we can conclude that our approach has a merit towards our aims. Firstly, the 82% score in the first evaluation where the users had to evaluate the answers based on their own CS, implies that our framework can provide knowledge for CS questions in a household environment. Additionally, the scores in the second evaluation show that the knowledge retrieval framework can be used as a baseline for evaluating other frameworks.

As for future work, we are planning to extend the scheme of the ontology with spatial information about objects, for example *soap is usually found near sink, sponge, bathtub, shower, shampoo*. Also, we plan to broaden the part of the framework which returns general knowledge about objects, by extracting knowledge from more open web knowledge graphs, in addition to DBpedia. Finally, we aim to extend the Semantic Matching Algorithm by obtaining information from other ontologies.

Acknowledgment. This project has received funding from the Hellenic Foundation for Research and Innovation (HFRI) and the General Secretariat for Research and Technology (GSRT), under grant agreement No 188.

References

1. Beetz, M., Bálint-Benczédi, F., Blodow, N., Nyga, D., Wiedemeyer, T., Marton, Z.C.: Roboscherlock: unstructured information processing for robot perception. In: 2015 IEEE International Conference on Robotics and Automation (ICRA), pp. 1549–1556. IEEE (2015)
2. Beetz, M., Beßler, D., Haidu, A., Pomarlan, M., Bozcuoğlu, A.K., Bartels, G.: Know rob 2.0–a 2nd generation knowledge processing framework for cognition-enabled robotic agents. In: 2018 IEEE International Conference on Robotics and Automation (ICRA), pp. 512–519. IEEE (2018)

3. Beßler, D., Koralewski, S., Beetz, M.: Knowledge representation for cognition-and learning-enabled robot manipulation. In: CogRob@ KR, pp. 11–19 (2018)

4. Bhattacharyya, R., Bhuyan, Z., Hazarika, S.M.: O-PrO: an ontology for object affordance reasoning. In: Basu, A., Das, S., Horain, P., Bhattacharya, S. (eds.) IHCI 2016. LNCS, vol. 10127, pp. 39–50. Springer, Cham (2017). https://doi.org/10.1007/978-3-319-52503-7_4

5. Bizer, C., et al.: DBpedia-a crystallization point for the web of data. Web Semant. Sci. Serv. Agents World Wide Web 7(3), 154–165 (2009)

6. Chernova, S., et al.: Situated Bayesian reasoning framework for robots operating in diverse everyday environments. In: Amato, N.M., Hager, G., Thomas, S., Torres-Torriti, M. (eds.) Robotics Research. Situated bayesian reasoning framework for robots operating in diverse everyday environments., vol. 10, pp. 353–369. Springer, Cham (2020). https://doi.org/10.1007/978-3-030-28619-4_29

7. Daruna, A., Liu, W., Kira, Z., Chetnova, S.: RoboCSE: robot common sense embedding. In: 2019 International Conference on Robotics and Automation (ICRA), pp. 9777–9783. IEEE (2019)

8. Fischer, L., et al.: Which tool to use? grounded reasoning in everyday environments with assistant robots. In: CogRob@ KR, pp. 3–10 (2018)

9. Gouidis, F., Vassiliades, A., Patkos, T., Argyros, A., Bassiliades, N., Plexousakis, D.: A review on intelligent object perception methods combining knowledge-based reasoning and machine learning. arXiv preprint arXiv:1912.11861 (2019)

10. Hepp, M.: GoodRelations: an ontology for describing products and services offers on the web. In: Gangemi, A., Euzenat, J. (eds.) EKAW 2008. LNCS (LNAI), vol. 5268, pp. 329–346. Springer, Heidelberg (2008). https://doi.org/10.1007/978-3-540-87696-0_29

11. Hitzler, P., Gangemi, A., Janowicz, K.: Ontology Engineering with Ontology Design Patterns: Foundations and Applications, vol. 25. IOS Press (2016)

12. Icarte, R.T., Baier, J.A., Ruz, C., Soto, A.: How a general-purpose commonsense ontology can improve performance of learning-based image retrieval. arXiv preprint arXiv:1705.08844 (2017)

13. Jäger, G., Mueller, C.A., Thosar, M., Zug, S., Birk, A.: Towards robot-centric conceptual knowledge acquisition. arXiv preprint arXiv:1810.03583 (2018)

14. Joulin, A., Grave, E., Bojanowski, P., Douze, M., Jégou, H., Mikolov, T.: Fasttext. zip: Compressing text classification models. arXiv preprint arXiv:1612.03651 (2016)

15. Kendall, E.F., McGuinness, D.L.: Ontology engineering. Synth. Lect. Semant. Web Theory Technol. 9(1), 1–102 (2019)

16. Lemaignan, S., Warnier, M., Sisbot, E.A., Clodic, A., Alami, R.: Artificial cognition for social human-robot interaction: an implementation. Artif. Intell. 247, 45–69 (2017)

17. Liao, Y.H., Puig, X., Boben, M., Torralba, A., Fidler, S.: Synthesizing environment-aware activities via activity sketches. In: Proceedings of the IEEE Conference on Computer Vision and Pattern Recognition, pp. 6291–6299 (2019)

18. Liu, H., Singh, P.: ConceptNet–a practical commonsense reasoning tool-kit. BT Technol. J. 22(4), 211–226 (2004)

19. McGuinness, D.L., Van Harmelen, F., et al.: Owl web ontology language overview. W3C Recomm. 10(10), 2004 (2004)

20. Meditskos, G., Kontopoulos, E., Vrochidis, S., Kompatsiaris, I.: Converness: Ontology-driven conversational awareness and context understanding in multimodal dialogue systems. Expert Systems (2019)

21. Pennington, J., Socher, R., Manning, C.: Glove: global vectors for word representation. In: Proceedings of the 2014 Conference on Empirical Methods in Natural Language Processing (EMNLP), pp. 1532–1543 (2014)

22. Salinas Pinacho, L., Wich, A., Yazdani, F., Beetz, M.: Acquiring knowledge of object arrangements from human examples for household robots. In: Trollmann, F., Turhan, A.-Y. (eds.) KI 2018. LNCS (LNAI), vol. 11117, pp. 131–138. Springer, Cham (2018). https://doi.org/10.1007/978-3-030-00111-7_12

23. Puig, X., et al.: Virtualhome: simulating household activities via programs. In: Proceedings of the IEEE Conference on Computer Vision and Pattern Recognition, pp. 8494–8502 (2018)

24. Radinger, A., Rodriguez-Castro, B., Stolz, A., Hepp, M.: BauDataWeb: the Austrian building and construction materials market as linked data. In: Proceedings of the 9th International Conference on Semantic Systems, pp. 25–32. ACM (2013)

25. Ramirez-Amaro, K., Beetz, M., Cheng, G.: Transferring skills to humanoid robots by extracting semantic representations from observations of human activities. Artif. Intell. **247**, 95–118 (2017)

26. Rong, X.: word2vec parameter learning explained. arXiv preprint arXiv:1411.2738 (2014)

27. Ruiz-Sarmiento, J.R., Galindo, C., Gonzalez-Jimenez, J.: Exploiting semantic knowledge for robot object recognition. Knowl.-Based Syst. **86**, 131–142 (2015)

28. Sanfilippo, E.M.: Feature-based product modelling: an ontological approach. Int. J. Comput. Integr. Manuf. **31**(11), 1097–1110 (2018)

29. Saxena, A., Jain, A., Sener, O., Jami, A., Misra, D.K., Koppula, H.S.: Robobrain: Large-scale knowledge engine for robots. arXiv preprint arXiv:1412.0691 (2014)

30. Strapparava, C., Valitutti, A., et al.: Wordnet affect: an affective extension of wordnet. In: LREC, vol. 4, p. 40. CiteSeer (2004)

31. Tenorth, M., Beetz, M.: Representations for robot knowledge in the KnowRob framework. Artif. Intell. **247**, 151–169 (2017)

32. Wagner, A., Rüppel, U.: BPO: the building product ontology for assembled products. In: Proceedings of the 7th Linked Data in Architecture and Construction workshop (LDAC 2019)', Lisbon, Portugal (2019)

33. Wiedemeyer, T., Bálint-Benczédi, F., Beetz, M.: Pervasive'calm'perception for autonomous robotic agents. In: Proceedings of the 2015 International Conference on Autonomous Agents and Multiagent Systems. International Foundation for Autonomous Agents and Multiagent Systems, pp. 871–879 (2015)

34. Yang, G., Wang, S., Yang, J.: Desire-driven reasoning for personal care robots. IEEE Access **7**, 75203–75212 (2019)

35. Young, J., Basile, V., Kunze, L., Cabrio, E., Hawes, N.: Towards lifelong object learning by integrating situated robot perception and semantic web mining. In: Proceedings of the Twenty-second European Conference on Artificial Intelligence, pp. 1458–1466. IOS Press (2016)

36. Young, J., et al.: Making sense of indoor spaces using semantic web mining and situated robot perception. In: Blomqvist, E., Hose, K., Paulheim, H., Ławrynowicz, A., Ciravegna, F., Hartig, O. (eds.) ESWC 2017. LNCS, vol. 10577, pp. 299–313. Springer, Cham (2017). https://doi.org/10.1007/978-3-319-70407-4_39

Semantic Annotation, Representation and Linking of Survey Data

Felix Bensmann[1]([✉]), Andrea Papenmeier[1], Dagmar Kern[1], Benjamin Zapilko[1], and Stefan Dietze[1,2,3]

[1] GESIS - Leibniz Institute for the Social Sciences, 50667 Cologne, Germany
{felix.bensmann,andrea.papenmeier,dagmar.kern,benjamin.zapilko,
stefan.dietze}@gesis.org
[2] Heinrich-Heine-University Düsseldorf, 40225 Düsseldorf, Germany
[3] L3S Research Center, 30167 Hannover, Germany
http://www.gesis.org

Abstract. Semantic technologies offer significant potential for improving data search applications. Ongoing work thrives to equip data catalogs with new semantic search features to supplement existing keyword search and browsing capabilities. In particular within the social sciences, searching and reusing data is essential to foster efficient research. In this paper, we introduce an approach and experimental results aimed at improving interoperability and findability of social sciences survey items. Our contributions include a conceptual model for semantically representing survey items and questions, detailing meaningful dimensions of items, as well as experimental results geared towards the automated prediction of such item features using state-of-the-art machine learning models. Dimensions of interest include, for instance, references to geolocation and time periods or the scope and style of particular questions. We define classification tasks using neural and traditional machine learning models combined with sentence structure features. Applications of our work include semantic and faceted search for questions as part of our GESIS Search. We also provide the lifted data as a knowledge graph via a SPARQL endpoint for further reuse and sharing.

Keywords: Question feature extraction · Social sciences survey data · Semantic data modelling · Natural language processing

1 Introduction

In the social sciences, questionnaire-based survey programs are the instrument of choice to collect information from a particular population. This survey data usually comprises attitudes, behaviours and factual information. To collect survey data, a research team usually composes a dedicated questionnaire for a population group and collects the data in personal interviews, telephone interviews, or online surveys. As this process is very complex and time-consuming, social scientists have a strong need for re-using both actual survey results for

© The Author(s) 2020
E. Blomqvist et al. (Eds.): SEMANTiCS 2020, LNCS 12378, pp. 53–69, 2020.
https://doi.org/10.1007/978-3-030-59833-4_4

secondary analysis [8] as well as well-designed and constructed survey items, e.g. specific questions. In Germany, GESIS - Leibniz Institute for the Social Sciences[1] is a major data provider that gathers, archives and provides survey data to researchers from all over the world. Datasets are searchable through GESIS Search[2] or gesisDataSearch[3]. Current research on social scientists' information needs indicates an increasing need for re-using survey data [17] and ongoing work already focuses on improving search applications with semantics e.g. from the users' perspective [12].

A crucial factor in the process of finding and identifying relevant survey data is the quality of available metadata. Metadata includes general information like title, date of collection, primary investigators, or sample, but also more specific information about the study's content like an abstract, topic classifications and keywords. So far, these metadata help to find a study of interest but they are less helpful if a researcher is interested in finding specific questions or variables. While a question is the text that is used to collect answers, variables contain the expression of the answers' characteristics. For example, the fictitious question "What is your attitude towards the European Union?" has the variable "AttiduteEU" which could have the characteristics (1) negative, (2) neutral, or (3) positive. Currently, no dedicated vocabularies are used for capturing the semantics of variables or items, for instance, their scope, nature or georeferences (EU in this case).

A common way for researchers to find variables and questions is to first find suitable datasets. In a second step, they read exhaustive documentation to find concrete questions or variables that fit their research question. For comparing variables and finding similar variables, this process has to be repeated. Recently introduced variable search systems[4] address this issue by providing a way to search for questions and variables with a common text-based search approach. However, the intention of a question or the concept to be measured are often not directly verbalized in its textual description.

In this paper, we examine how a variable's content can be described more expressively, using state-of-the-art semantic technologies. Therefore, we focus on extracting and representing additional information from a question that go beyond tagging the questions with keywords and topics. Our approach is based on the ofness and aboutness concept of survey data introduced by [10]. While ofness refers to the literal question wording, which often reveals information about the topic of a question, the aboutness relates to the latent content. In our work, we focus on the aboutness aspects. This includes, for instance, the scope and nature of a question, e.g. whether the question asks for opinions or about a fact about the interviewee's life.

The so called question features are designed to complement each other and are formally modeled as RDF(S) data model. We also introduce experiments for

---

[1] https://www.gesis.org.

[2] https://search.gesis.org/.

[3] https://datasearch.gesis.org/start.

[4] like ICPSR https://www.icpsr.umich.edu [25], GESIS Search https://search.gesis.org [14], paneldata.org https://paneldata.org/.

supervised classification models able to automatically predict question features. As the focus of our work is more on the question features and their systematic we started with established classifiers leaving more recent approaches for future work. Experiments are conducted on a real-world corpus of frequently used survey questions, consisting of 6500 distinct questions. For each question, we extract the question features by using a variety of text classification approaches, e.g., neural networks like LSTM. In addition, we generated a knowledge graph (KG) and publish the results via a dedicated SPARQL endpoint[5].

Our main contributions can be summarized as followed: (1) We provide a taxonomy of question features and (2) a comprehensive data model describing the questions and the features in relation to each other. Finally, (3) we provide methods and first results for the prediction of one question feature, i.e. for populating a knowledge base of expressive question metadata.

The paper is structured as follows. First, we provide the related work in Sect. 2 and elaborate the design of the question features and the data model in Sect. 3. Afterwards, in Sect. 4, we describe our experiments on extracting the "Information type" question feature before we eventually close discussing application scenarios and draw a conclusion (Sect. 5).

2   Related Work

In this section, we discuss related work, including available survey data catalog systems, relevant RDF vocabularies for model design and methods for feature extraction.

Some notable providers of social science survey data in Germany and internationally are GESIS, LifBi(NEPS)[6], SOEP/DIW[7], pairfam[8] and ICPSR. These institutions allow their customers access to data and documentation on different levels. Smaller institutions are known for a narrow set of datasets, they do not host complex online catalogs but provide study documentation as HTML or PDFs online. However, sometimes they cooperate with larger institutions or consortiums that host their datasets. SOEP and pairfam, for example, take part in panaldata.org a data catalog for variables, questions, concepts, publications and topics. It provides text based search. Larger institutions like GESIS and ICPSR host large catalogs for study level data and sub-studylevel data. GESIS' GESIS Search and ICPSR's data portal are two examples for more complete search applications. Yet, to our knowledge there is no example of a variable catalog system that uses expressive and formally represented question features like the ones presented in this paper.

For our data model, we investigated related RDF vocabularies. [13] outlines best practices to consider when publishing data as Linked Open Data by e.g. reusing established vocabularies. Relevant work is found in vocabularies

---

[5] http://data.gesis.org/questionfeaturessample/site.

[6] https://www.neps-data.de/Mainpage.

[7] https://www.diw.de/en/soep.

[8] https://www.pairfam.de/en/.

describing scientific data e.g. the DDI RDF discovery vocabulary[9] [2,3]. It is based on the Data Documentation Initiative (DDI) metadata standard, which is an acknowledged standard to describe survey data in the social sciences. DataCube[10] focuses on statistical data. Large cross-domain vocabularies of relevance include Schema.org[11] and DBpedia[12]. Further candidates are upper-level vocabularies like DOLCE-Lite-Plus[13], as they serve more general terms and are not focused at specific domains.

With respect to methodological work on classification of short text, e.g. for predicting question features, approaches include the ones surveyed by [1], where the authors provide a survey on text classification examples for different tasks like "News filtering and Organization", "Document Organization and Retrieval", "Opinion Mining" or "Email Classification and Spam Filtering" applying various approaches e.g. "Decision Trees", "Pattern (Rule)-based Classifiers", "SVM Classifiers" and many more. The authors elaborate also on the experimental setups and best practices. Similar work can also be found in [20]. The survey presented in [24] elaborates on the special aspects of short texts and popular work on classifiers using semantic analysis, ensemble short text classification etc. is introduced. In [5] the authors present an approach specialized for short text classification leveraging external knowledge and deep neural networks. A famous short text corpus and target of many classification/extraction tasks is Twitter[14]. Our work relates for example to the extraction of specific dimensions e.g. sentiments [21] or events [27]. While individual approaches certainly overlap with ours, as they work on (rather arbitrary) short texts, our setup leverages specifics of survey questions which allows to compose our question features in a systematic way so that they complement each others and serve a common goal, i.e. better performance in a search system.

3   Semantic Features of Survey Questions

Before we introduce our taxonomy of question features, we give a closer description of survey questions.

3.1   Survey Questions

A question in a questionnaire is described through a question text and predefined answer categories[15]. Figure 1 depicts three example questions. In some cases, when a group of questions differs in only the object they refer to, questionnaire designers assemble these in item batteries, where the items share question text

---

[9] http://rdf-vocabulary.ddialliance.org/discovery.html.
[10] https://www.w3.org/TR/vocab-data-cube/.
[11] http://schema.org.
[12] http://dbpedia.org/ontology/.
[13] https://www.w3.org/2001/sw/BestPractices/WNET/DLP3941_daml.html.
[14] https://twitter.com.
[15] We do not consider open questions at the moment, as there are none in the data.

and answer categories. An example can be seen in Fig. 1 (question in the center). A variable corresponds to either a complete question when there is only one answer available, or a question item. In the remainder of the paper and in our dataset, we treat questions having several items as separate instances and refer to them as "question-item pairs". Questions without items are likewise a single question instance.

How is the head of state selected?	Do you think that the introduction of the new technologies in Canada over the next few years will make work …	
0 Not applicable; head of state not indirectly elected	… much more interesting	1
	… a little more interesting	2
		3
2 Lowe chamber		4
3 Upper chamber		5
4 Both chambers		8
9 Missing		

How frequently would you say you buy each of the following types of fishery and aquaculture products?					
	Often	From time to time	Rarely	Never	DK
Loose products (e.g. from the fishmonger's slab)	1	2	3	4	5
Pre-packed products	1	2	3	4	5

Fig. 1. Example questions. CSES 2015 (left), ISSP 1997 (center) and Eurobarometer 2018 (right) [9, 16, 26]

Survey questions are not necessarily questions in the grammatical sense, i.e. a single sentence with a question mark at the end. Many questions incorporate introductory texts and definitions for clarification. Additionally, they are often formulated as requests for the respondent or they are prompts for supplement. Meaning they are formulated as the first part of a statement, stopping with "…" and leaving the second part to the respondent to complete. The question instances in our dataset have between one and 171 words with 29 words on average.

Other properties documenting variables are an identifier, a label, interviewer instructions, keywords, topic classification, encoding in the dataset and more.

3.2 A Taxonomy of Question Features

We assume that a search session for a question starts with a topic or keyword search and is subsequently refined through the use of facets. Our taxonomy presented in the following focuses on the facets. Therefor it does not include features regarding the actual topic which can be extracted by e.g. topic modelling. For our semantic description, we identified recurrent patterns in survey questions through literature [23], elaboration with domain experts as well as brainstorming. We looked into more than 500 questions and question-item pairs from over 200 studies. From this we compiled an initial list of potential question features to be discussed individually with two experts who we trust. Our foremost interest was to identify relevant filter criteria for social scientists. Subsequently, we oriented us along the requirements needed for use cases such as faceted search of items, questions or variables and identified some criteria any feature should adhere to. These include explicitness, distinctiveness, comprehensibility, a discrete value range (which may be described through a controlled vocabulary), meaningfulness, recurrence in our dataset, annotatability (practical[16]) and extractability.

We came up with a list of 11 question features involving features that describe the problem/task given to the respondent, e.g. the scene depicted, statements that can be made about the information asked, the tone and complexity of language or the nature of the object of the question.

Our features are presented in the following. The list names the question feature and provides a definition and the value range. For instance the question feature Time reference captures whether a question refers to the past, present or future of the respondents life, or whether a hypothetical scenario is depicted. Depending on the situation more than one value could be correct. I. e. the Information type was designed to be mutual exclusive. All question features are either of *- or 0..1- cardinality. The values are to be determined through individual approaches, e.g. a text classification or keyword matching, for example the value range for the question feature Geographic location is meant to correspond with the Geonames[17] gazetteer. For reasons of conciseness, we omitted the definitions of the allowed values in the list. They are however presented online along with the KG documentation.

Information type. The information type of a question characterizes which type of information the respondent is asked to state about the question object. Values: Evaluation (Sub-values: Willingness, Preference, Acceptance, Prediction, Assessment, Explanation), Fact (Sub-values: Demography, Participation, Activity, Decision, Use, Interaction, Behaviour, Life Events), Cognition (Sub-values: Emotion, Knowledge, Perception, Interest, Motivation, Believes, Understanding).

Focus. This feature characterizes the focus of the question object. Whether it is focused towards the respondent, another person or if it is wide as in a general question. Values: Self focus, External focus (Sub-values: Family/Member of family, Acquaintance, Affiliate, Public Person, Institution, Object focus/item focus, Event focus), Generic/universal focus and Self+external focus.

Time reference. Time reference characterizes the question's time reference wrt. past, present and future. Values: Past, Present, Future, Hypothetical - past, Hypothetical - present, Hypothetical - future.

Periodicity. Periodicity characterizes the duration and periodicity of the time the question refers to. Values: Point in time, Time span, Periodic point in time, Unspecific.

---

[16] A human annotator needs to be able to work out the correct annotation with reasonable effort. E.g., long or nested value ranges, rare and too specific or too similar terms need to be avoided.

[17] https://www.geonames.org/.

Information intimacy. Information intimacy characterizes the sensitivity of the requested information with respect to personal life. Values: Private, Public.

Relative location. The relative location states a location that is mentioned which is not described by a geographic name but by its meaning for the respondent. Values: Without, Apartment/Flat, Neighborhood/Street, Municipality/City, Region, Country, Continent, World, Place of work, Journey, Stays abroad.

Geographic location. The name of a geographic location if mentioned. Values: <Continent>, <Countries>, <Region>, <Government region>, Others, Without, Unspecific, Mixed/Multiple

Knowledge specificity. Describes the specificity of the knowledge that is required to answer the question according to the origin of that knowledge. Values: School, Daily life, Special knowledge.

Quantification. This feature captures the quantification of the answer. As opposed to Information type it is more concrete and close to physical quantity. Values: Frequency, Date time, Time dimension, Spatial expansion, Mass, Amount, Level of agreement, Boolean, Rating, Naming/Denomination, Order, Comparative.

Language tone. Language tone characterizes the degree of formality or tone that is applied in the question. Values: Colloquial language, Formal language, Jargon/technical language.

Language complexity. Language complexity characterizes the complexity of phrasing applied in the question. Values: Simple language, Moderate language level, Raised language level.

3.3   Data Model and Vocabulary

Our model connects to the DDI-RDF Discovery vocabulary (DISCO) [2,3]. It is an RDF representation of the Data Documentation Initiative (DDI) data model, an established standard for study metadata, maintained by the DDI Alliance[18]. While in DISCO the focus is set on a formal documentation of a questionnaire and its questions, our model extends the survey questions by a conceptual representation with the content dimensions (question features) described in the list above. We arranged the question features in groups for a better overview and to be able to link and reuse related and similar question characteristics in the future. When designing the model, we tried to identify terms in established vocabularies like those mentioned in related work in order to follow best practices and facilitate reuse and interpretation of the data. Since the scope of our model is specialised towards the social sciences, reflecting very particular dimensions and features, for a large number of classes and properties in our model no adequate terms could be found in existing vocabularies. In Fig. 2 we present the designed model on a conceptual level.

---

[18] https://ddialliance.org/.

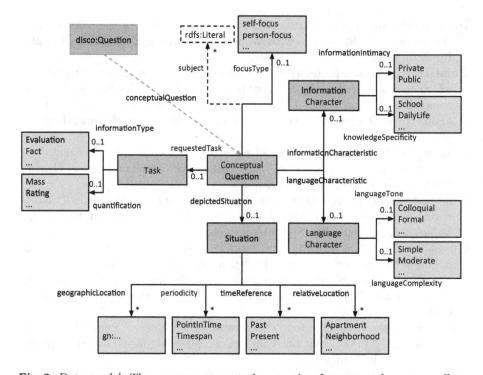

Fig. 2. Data model. The arrows represent the question features and groups, yellow boxes indicate the value range for a question feature, orange boxes indicates a group. The gray and the white box help to connect to the context. (Color figure online)

Our dataset is available online[19] along with a SPARQL endpoint and webpage describing the data and providing example queries.

4   Annotation and Enrichment

In total, there are 165 184 machine readable and sufficiently documented variables (i.e. questions or question-item pairs) available. The 101 554 variables having an English question text are included in our data set. To create a gold standard, we drew uniformly at random 6500 variables for manual annotation from this dataset. GESIS Search[20] provides access to all studies and their documentations involved in our work.

4.1   Manual Annotation

In a first step, we decided to focus on the feature Information type. We recruited an annotator based on annotation experience and knowledge about social science terminology to annotate this feature type. Before the annotation, the label

---

[19] http://data.gesis.org/questionfeaturessample/site.
[20] https://search.gesis.org, category research data.

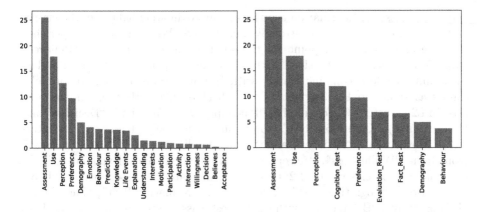

Fig. 3. Distribution of Information type L2 labels, original (left) and merged (right)

categories were explained to the annotator. In a training phase with 100 question instances (excluded from the final data set), annotations that the annotator perceived as difficult were discussed with the authors.

The custom web interface guided the annotation process by displaying the question text, item text (if available), and the answer options. The annotator selected exactly two labels for each question, one label for Information type L1 and one label for L2. Once the annotator selected a label for L1, the corresponding sub-values (L2) are presented to reduce cognitive load and avoid mistakes. For each question instance, the annotator reported her level of confidence on a scale of 0 ("not confident at all") to 10 ("very confident"). In total, 511 question instances were omitted due to an annotator-certainty of under 4. The final annotated dataset, therefore, consists of 5989 question instances.

At the end of the process, the annotator annotated 1200 question instances a second time to calculate the test-retest reliability. Cohen's kappa coefficient reaches a substantial self-agreement of .72 for L1 and .64 for L2, a sufficient level of reliability to trust the consistency of the annotator.

4.2 Automatic Prediction

Based on the provided annotations for the Information type, we can extract this question feature automatically from the natural language text of the question and the item text, if applicable. In our case, predicting the question features described in Sect. 3 represents a multi-class classification task. We tested and compared multiple classifiers on this task each for L1 and L2: LSTM [11], RandomForest [4], Multinomial Naive Bayes [18], Linear Support Vector Machines [7] and Logistic Regression [15]. We also took different kinds of input features into account: Word sequences and text structure.

The annotated values for L1 are distributed as follows: 42.08% Evaluation, 33.30% Fact and 24.62% Cognition. For L2, we provide the original distribution in Fig. 3 (left). The y-axis shows the percentages of relative occurrence.

While the classes of Information type L1 are approximately balanced, the classes of Information type L2 are strongly imbalanced. We assume by experience that the amount of data points in the smaller classes of L2 (e.g. "Believes" with 15 instances, or "Decision" with 39 instances) is too low to train a classifier and therefore combine classes with insufficient instances into umbrella classes as shown in Fig. 3 (right). For each class in L1, there is an umbrella class in L2: "Fact_Rest" (combining "Participation", "Activity", "Decision" and "Life Events"), "Cognition_Rest" (combining "Emotion", "Knowledge", "Interest", "Motivation", "Believes" and "Understanding") and "Evaluation_Rest" (combining "Willingness", "Acceptance", "Prediction" and "Explanation"). In the final set of classes for L2 there are nine labels: "Assessment", "Use", "Perception", "Cognition_Rest", "Preference", "Evaluation_Rest", "Fact_Rest", "Demography", "Behaviour", with the biggest class ("Assessment") having 1523 instances, and the smallest ("Behaviour") containing 221 samples. The umbrella classes of L2 are currently not part of the data model (cf. Sect. 3.3) as the respective L1 class can be used instead e.g. "Cognition" for "Cognition_Rest".

Using Word Sequences. As natural language can be understood as a sequence of words, modern sequence models are a good fit to classify natural languages. Long-Short Term Memory (LSTM) models have shown to outperform other sequential neural network architectures [11] when applied to context-free languages such as natural language. We therefore employ an LSTM architecture to classify the natural language questions in our data set and will subsequently refer to this approach as seq_lstm.

We implemented the LSTM network using Keras' [6] sequential model in Python 3.6. The model has a three layer architecture, with an embeddings input layer (embeddings with dimension 100), an LSTM layer (100 nodes, dropout and recurrent dropout at 0.2), and a dense output layer with softmax activation. The model is trained with categorical cross-entropy loss and optimised on accuracy (equals micro-f1 in a single class classification task).

The embeddings layer uses the complete training data to compute word vectors with 100 dimensions. The question instances are preprocessed by removing all punctuation besides the apostrophe and converting all characters to lower case. For tokenisation, the texts are split on whitespaces. Since the input sequences to the embeddings layer need to be of equal length, we pad the sentences to a fixed length of 50 words by appending empty word tokens to the start of the sequence. On average, the question-item sequences contain 29 words, with a standard deviation of 16 words. Sequences longer than 50 words (8% of the question-item pairs, whereof 50% are shorter than 60 words) are cut off at the end to fit the fixed input length.

Using Text Structure. For this second approach, we used the structure of the question texts as input for our models. The idea behind this approach is the assumption of a dependency existing between the sentence structure of a question and the Information type.

Expecting the item text to provide valuable information for predicting the Information type through the text structure, we concatenated question text and item when an item was present. We extracted the structure from the otherwise unprocessed text by using a Part-of-speech (POS) parser to shallow parse (also referred to as light parsing or chunking) the question instances into a tree of typed chunks. From this we used the chunk types except for the leaf nodes (the POS tags) to define a feature vector where each component represents the number of occurrences of a specific chunk type. There are 27 different chunk types.

For the actual parsing we choose the Stanford PCFG parser in version 3.9.2 [19] as it is well-known and tolerant towards misspellings. However, some special cases in the phrasing introduce noise. Some expressions miss expressiveness as they refer to information presented in a previous question ("How is it in this case?") or in the answer categories ("Would you ..."). Furthermore, misspellings and similar errors introduce additional noise. Since the parser was able to provide a structure for all samples we did not have to exclude any samples. Leaving all 5989 samples for use.

We started testing using standard classifiers RandomForest (str_rf), Multinomial Naive Bayes (str_mnb), Linear Support Vector Machines (str_svc) and Logistic Regression (str_logreg) from the scikit-learn [22] library for Python. For each model we performed grid hyperparameter tuning on the training set with 5-fold cross-validation. We report parameters deviating from the default configuration. For str_svc we used C=0.5, max_iter=5000 and 'ovr'=multi_class mode. For str_rf n_estimators=200, max_features=3 and max_depth=50 was used. Again for str_logreg we applied C=10 and max_iter=5000. Finally str_mnb was used with alpha=3.

4.3   Evaluation Setup

For evaluating, we employ five-folds cross-validation with 80% training and 20% test set split and use the manual annotations as ground truth. For the best performing approach for predicting Information types L1 and L2, we also present and discuss the confusion matrices.

4.4   Results

Table 1 displays the results for the L1 and L2 Information types. The first column states the name of the respective approach and model. The following two columns contain micro-f1 and macro-f1 for the L1 Information types and the remaining two columns do the same for the L2 Information types.

As we can see in Table 1, L1 seq_lstm has the highest micro-f1 score with 0.7640 followed by the group of str_-approaches which range between 0.5305 and 0.6287. The macro-f1 follows the same pattern with seq_lstm at 0.7455 and the others again grouped together and more than 0.17 points beneath. This is similar for L2 where seq_lstm again has the best micro-f1 and macro-f1 scores at 0.4793 and 0.482.

Table 1. Results of L1 and L2 Information type extraction

Approach	L1		L2	
	micro-f1	macro-f1	micro-f1	macro-f1
seq_lstm	**0.7640**	**0.7455**	**0.4793**	**0.482**
str_svc	0.5437	0.524	0.3444	0.2610
str_rf	0.6287	0.5751	0.4578	0.3754
str_logreg	0.5454	0.5329	0.3386	0.2844
str_mnb	0.5305	0.526	0.3377	0.2656

Our anticipated usage scenario is a facetted search in a data search portal i.e. the GESIS Search. Here users will be presented the question features as facets and be allowed to use them to define their search request more precisely. Due to the infinite ways to formulate questions (and to specify classes), sometimes the assignment of a question to a class is ambiguous, also when done manually. Different users may associate a certain question with a different class and may still be correct. Thus, our intuition is that an F1 score of 0.7 could be counted as suitable.

For L1 seq_lstm matches this goal. Also the str_-approaches are not out of range. However, results for L2 will need to be improved. Performance limiting factors may be low expressiveness of features and too similar classes. Given the high number of classes for L2 we are content with the models' performances, however for the use case it might be better to merge some of the classes. For closer elaboration we present the confusion matrices in the Figs. 4 and 5.

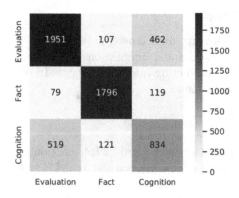

Fig. 4. Confusion matrix for LSTM classifier on Information type L1

In the diagrams, the predicted classes are on the X-axis and the actual classes are on the Y-axis. Both confusion matrices show little mispredictions of "Fact" or "Fact"-subclasses. In contrast, "Evaluation" and "Cognition" get confused

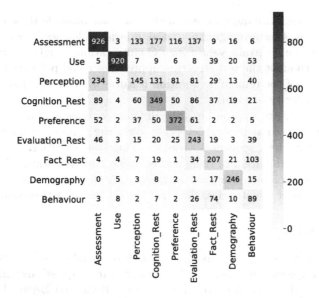

Fig. 5. Confusion matrix for LSTM classifier on Information type L2

more often. Especially in Fig. 5 "Assessment" (sub-class of "Evaluation") gets mispredicted as "Perception" (sub-class of "Cognition") and vice-versa. Also, a notable fraction of "Assessment" is confused with "Cognition_Rest". Looking at the concerned classes' labels, it is apparent that the concepts they represent are also for humans not easy to tell apart.

To test for this we conducted a small experiment for inter-annotator agreement where we reannotated 200 of the samples through two extra annotators. It resulted in an average Cohen's κ of 0.61 for L1 and 0.53 for L2 and Krippendorf's α of 0.55 and 0.44. These values, except for $\kappa = 0.61$, substantiate the notion that the task is even for humans not trivial. Which again indicates an indistinct design of the Information type classes, especially for L2. Supposedly a pilot study including multiple human annotators could help to define a clearer set of classes. However, classes should have intuitive denominations as complex artificial classes are hard to communicate to the users. Another way to overcome this could be to redesign the task as multi-class classification task. This however would come at the cost of simplicity for the user. Anyway, for this experiment the numbers show validity of our approach to a certain degree. An interesting question in this context will be to determine how the results change if the threshold for the confidence score for the inclusion of annotated questions into the dataset is raised.

A few things that could be improved are e.g. the selection of features for the str.-approaches which is rather sparse at the moment i.e. the feature vector might not carry enough information for the classifiers. Hence, a solution could be to extend the feature selection by the inclusion of signal words. E.g. "think", "find", "believe" may indicate opinions.

Once there are more question feature extractions available these can be used as input for each other leveraging potential interdependencies between then, e.g. in "Fact" questions certain values for "Quantification" might be more likely. Following the thought the test structure approaches could potentially be reused to extract some of the remaining question features directly, e.g. Language tone, Language complexity or Focus.

Str_* and seq_lstm approaches take different/complementary kinds of features into account. That is, str_* leverages solely the grammatical structure of a sentence, seq_lstm uses sequences of words. Thus, our intuition is that there is potential for a combination of them e.g. by using the predictions of both types of the classifiers as input into a meta-classifier. A closer analysis on the nature of mispredictions of the str_-classifiers will be conducted in this context.

5 Conclusion

We present an approach to support the search of social science survey data by defining and implementing methods to annotate survey questions with semantic features. These dimensions complement existing topic and keyword extraction and allow for a finer grained semantic description.

We defined the dimensions as a taxonomy of question features (contribution 1), and designed a data model to describe the annotated data with the dimensions and lifted it together with the variable descriptions to RDF for re-use in other use-cases (contribution 2). Eventually, we examined approaches to predict the first question feature, the Information type, by means of classification tasks and present word sequences in combination with LSTM as a promising way (contribution 3). However, we consider combining it with one of the text structure approaches in the future.

Our question feature model offers many possibilities for applications. It is especially designed to be integrated in a facet filter scenario, but provides also multiple options for use in data linking, sharing and discovery scenarios. We target the GESIS Search https://search.gesis.org for a possible deployment. It is an integrated search system allowing search of multiple resource types including "Research data", "Publications", "Instruments & Tools", "GESIS Webpages", "GESIS Library" and "Variables & Questions". The current filter offers the facets *year*, *source* and *study title* for the category of "Variables & Questions". These will be complemented with our Information type feature. Besides lowering the assessment times for searchers per study, it could also improve re-use frequency and findability especially for less known datasets. Accordingly, less-experienced users may find it easier to orient themselves. Given that an already annotated training set can be reused, data providers in turn benefit from reduced efforts in variable documentation since this can be done automatically.

We are positive that there are additional use cases where a subset of our features can be reused to semantically describe textual contents. For example, short descriptions or titles of e.g. images can be annotated with the situation features. Also, language and knowledge features are applicable for these scenarios and can help to assess a text by getting to know the audience.

In future work, we plan to annotate and predict more features and fine tune the presented approach. Furthermore, a user study is planned to test for fitness in terms of (a) comprehensiveness of the facet and its values, (b) acceptance of the concept of the Information type and (c) trust in the accuracy of the annotation. A revision of the question feature design might still be necessary in order to fit user acceptance.

Funding. This work was partly funded by the DFG, grant no. 388815326; the VACOS project at GESIS.

References

1. Aggarwal, C.C., Zhai, C.X.: A survey of text classification algorithms. In: Aggarwal, C., Zhai, C.X. (eds.) Mining Text Data, pp. 163–222. Springer, Heidelberg (2012). https://doi.org/10.1007/978-1-4614-3223-4_6
2. Bosch, T., Gregory, A., Cyganiak, R., Wackerow, J.: DDI-RDF discovery vocabulary: a metadata vocabulary for documenting research and survey data. In: CEUR Workshop Proceedings, vol. 996 (2013)
3. Bosch, T., Zapilko, B., Wackerow, J., Gregory, A.: Towards the discovery of person-level data reuse of vocabularies and related use cases. In: CEUR Workshop Proceedings, vol. 1549 (2013)
4. Breiman, L.: Random forests. Mach. Learn. **45**, 5–32 (2001). https://doi.org/10.1023/A:1010933404324
5. Chen, J., Hu, Y., Liu, J., Xiao, Y., Jiang, H.: Deep short text classification with knowledge powered attention. Proc. AAAI Conf. Artif. Intell. **33**, 6252–6259 (2019). https://doi.org/10.1609/aaai.v33i01.33016252
6. Chollet, F., et al.: Keras (2015). https://keras.io
7. Cortes, C., Vapnik, V.: Support-vector networks. Mach. Learn. **20**, 273–297 (1995). https://doi.org/10.1023/A:1022627411411
8. Curty, R.G.: Factors influencing research data reuse in the social sciences: an exploratory study. Int. J. Digit. Curation **11**(1), 96–117 (2016)
9. European Commission, Brussels: Eurobarometer 89.3 (2018), (2019). https://doi.org/10.4232/1.13212
10. Friedrich, T., Siegers, P.: The ofness and aboutness of survey data: improved indexing of social science questionnaires. In: Wilhelm, A.F.X., Kestler, H.A. (eds.) Analysis of Large and Complex Data. SCDAKO, pp. 629–638. Springer, Cham (2016). https://doi.org/10.1007/978-3-319-25226-1_54
11. Gers, F., Schmidhuber, E.: LSTM recurrent networks learn simple context-free and context-sensitive languages. IEEE Trans. Neural Netw. **12**(6), 1333–1340 (2001). https://doi.org/10.1109/72.963769
12. Gregory, K.M., Cousijn, H., Groth, P., Scharnhorst, A., Wyatt, S.: Understanding data search as a socio-technical practice. J. Inf. Sci. (2019). https://doi.org/10.1177/0165551519837182
13. Heath, T., Bizer, C.: Linked Data: Evolving the Web into a Global Data Space, vol. 1. Morgan & Claypool, San Rafael (2011). https://doi.org/10.2200/S00334ED1V01Y201102WBE0010.2200/S00334ED1V01Y201102WBE0010.2200/S00334ED1V01Y201102WBE00

14. Hienert, D., Kern, D., Boland, K., Zapilko, B., Mutschke, P.: A digital library for research data and related information in the social sciences. In: 2019 ACM/IEEE Joint Conference on Digital Libraries (JCDL), pp. 148–157 (2019). https://doi.org/10.1109/JCDL.2019.00030

15. Hosmer Jr., D.W., Lemeshow, S., Sturdivant, R.X.: Applied Logistic Regression, vol. 398. Wiley, Hoboken (2013)

16. ISSP Research Group: International Social Survey Programme: Work Orientations II - ISSP 1997 (1999). https://doi.org/10.4232/1.3090

17. Kern, D., Hienert, D.: Understanding the information needs of social scientists in Germany. Proc. Assoc. Inf. Sci. Technol. **55**(1), 234–243 (2018). https://doi.org/10.1002/pra2.2018.14505501026

18. Kibriya, A.M., Frank, E., Pfahringer, B., Holmes, G.: Multinomial naive Bayes for text categorization revisited. In: Webb, G.I., Yu, X. (eds.) AI 2004. LNCS (LNAI), vol. 3339, pp. 488–499. Springer, Heidelberg (2004). https://doi.org/10.1007/978-3-540-30549-1_43

19. Klein, D., Manning, C.D.: Accurate unlexicalized parsing. In: Proceedings of the 41st Annual Meeting on Association for Computational Linguistics - ACL 2003, Morristown, NJ, USA, vol. 1, pp. 423–430. Association for Computational Linguistics (2003). https://doi.org/10.3115/1075096.1075150, http://portal.acm.org/citation.cfm?doid=1075096.1075150

20. Kowsari, K., Meimandi, K.J., Heidarysafa, M., Mendu, S., Barnes, L., Brown, D.: Text classification algorithms: a survey. Information (Switzerland) **10**(4), 1–68 (2019). https://doi.org/10.3390/info10040150

21. Narr, S., Hulfenhaus, M., Albayrak, S.: Language-independent Twitter sentiment analysis. Knowledge Discovery and Machine Learning (KDML), LWA pp. 12–14 (2012)

22. Pedregosa, F., et al.: Scikit-learn: machine learning in Python. J. Mach. Learn. Res. **12**, 2825–2830 (2011)

23. Porst, R.: Fragebogen : ein Arbeitsbuch. Array, VS Verl. für Sozialwiss., 2. aufl. edn. (2009)

24. Song, G., Ye, Y., Du, X., Huang, X., Bie, S.: Short text classification: a survey. J. Multimedia **9**(5), 635–643 (2014). https://doi.org/10.4304/jmm.9.5.635-643

25. Swanberg, S.: Inter-university consortium for political and social research (ICPSR). J. Med. Libr. Assoc. **105**(1), 106–107 (2017). https://doi.org/10.5195/jmla.2017.120. http://jmla.pitt.edu/ojs/jmla/article/view/120

26. The Comparative Study of Electoral Systems: CSES Module 2 Full Release (2015). https://doi.org/10.7804/cses.module2.2015-12-15

27. Wang, X., Zhu, F., Jiang, J., Li, S.: Real time event detection in Twitter. In: Wang, J., Xiong, H., Ishikawa, Y., Xu, J., Zhou, J. (eds.) Web-Age Information Management. WAIM 2013. Lecture Notes in Computer Science, vol. 7923, pp. 502–513. Springer, Heidelberg (2013). https://doi.org/10.1007/978-3-642-38562-9-51

QueDI: From Knowledge Graph Querying to Data Visualization

Renato De Donato[1], Martina Garofalo[2], Delfina Malandrino[1],
Maria Angela Pellegrino[1(✉)], Andrea Petta[1], and Vittorio Scarano[1]

[1] Dipartimento di Informatica, Università di Salerno, Fisciano, Italy
`rended83@gmail.com`, {`dmalandrino,mapellegrino,vitsca`}`@unisa.it`,
`andrpet@gmail.com`
[2] ACT OR S.r.l., Rome, Italy
`martina.garofalo@act-operationsresearch.com`

Abstract. While Open Data (OD) publishers are spur in providing data as Linked Open Data (LOD) to boost innovation and knowledge creation, the complexity of RDF querying languages, such as SPARQL, threatens their exploitation. We aim to help lay users (by focusing on experts in table manipulation, such as OD experts) in querying and exploiting LOD by taking advantage of our target users' expertise in table manipulation and chart creation.

We propose QueDI (Query Data of Interest), a question-answering and visualization tool that implements a scaffold transitional approach to 1) query LOD without being aware of SPARQL and representing results by data tables; 2) once reached our target user comfort zone, users can manipulate and 3) visually represent data by exportable and dynamic visualizations. The main novelty of our approach is the split of the querying phase in SPARQL query building and data table manipulation.

In this article, we present the QueDI operating mechanism, its interface supported by a guided use-case over DBpedia, and the evaluation of its accuracy and usability level.

Keywords: Knowledge graph · Query builder · Data visualization · SPARQL & SQL queries · Faceted search · Natural language queries

1 Introduction

Open Data (OD) providers mainly opt for publishing data by non-proprietary formats (such as CSV) [8]. As a publisher, it requires minimum effort due to the easiness of the data format, and, as a consumer, it provides free access to resources [3,4]. To fully benefit from OD, data should also provide their context to create new knowledge and enable data exploitation [3]. Therefore, data providers are strongly encouraged to move published datasets from 3-stars to 5-stars, i.e., to publish data in RDF format and interlink them to other resources to provide context [4]. 5-stars data are also referred to as Linked Open Data (LOD).

© The Author(s) 2020
E. Blomqvist et al. (Eds.): SEMANTiCS 2020, LNCS 12378, pp. 70–86, 2020.
https://doi.org/10.1007/978-3-030-59833-4_5

Among the several different definitions of a Knowledge Graph (KG), we adopt the definition according to a KG is achieved by attaching to LOD their schema (i.e., an ontology) [15]. LOD facilitate innovation and knowledge creation from the publishing perspective [3,4]. However, from the consumption point of view, LOD exploitation is threatened by the complexity of their querying languages. Even if SPARQL [22] has been recognized as the most common query language for RDF data, it proves to be too challenging, mainly for lay users [7,9].

The *problem* we aim to solve is how to help potential users of the semantic web in *easily* accessing LOD (without requiring the explicit usage of SPARQL) and in exploiting the retrieved data. We aim to mainly focus on experts in data table manipulation and chart creation. It is not a strong limitation since many data visualization tools start from CSV files (or in general data tables). Thus, we can refer to our target users as experts in data table manipulation, and we aim to guide them in manipulating LOD through their tabular representation.

We propose a *transitional approach* where users are guided from LOD querying to our target user comfort zone, i.e., a tabular representation of data, table manipulation, and chart generation. As a result, we implement this transitional approach in *QueDI* (Query Data of Interest) that allows users to build queries step-by-step with an auto-complete mechanism and to exploit retrieved results by exportable and dynamic visualizations. Users can query LOD without explicitly creating SPARQL queries, and it is not required any previous knowledge of queried data. Users can inspect the nature of data by inspection, using natural language (NL) and query building. Query builders are about trading off *usability* of the proposed mechanism and its *expressivity*. We opt for a faceted search interface (FSI) enhanced by a NL query to extract results that reply to users' requests and by modelling them as a table. By this approach, we cover Basic Graph Patterns (BGPs), such as path traversal, union, filters, negation, and optional patterns. The component that implements this approach (corresponding to the first step of our workflow) will be referred to as ELODIE (Extractor of Linked Open Data of IntErest) (pronounced elədē). When users are satisfied with the retrieved results, they can move to the second step of our workflow, i.e., the table manipulation, to perform aggregations, filtering, sorting; finally, they can represent knowledge by dynamic and exportable visualizations during the third and last step of our scaffolded approach. Therefore, by combining the expressivity of ELODIE and table manipulation, we cover SELECT queries which results can always be represented as a table, BGPs directly in SPARQL, sorting, GROUP BY, aggregation operators and filtering by table manipulation.

The Research Questions (RQs) we aim to reply are:

RQ1. *Does the proposed approach lose in accuracy?* We aim to compare our two-phase approach (SPARQL queries building and table manipulation) with the formulation of SPARQL queries only exploiting SPARQL query building.

RQ2. *Do lay users (users without technical skills in the Semantic Web technologies) consider usable the ELODIE operating mechanism and its interface?*

RQ3. *Are lay users able to quickly learn how to exploit ELODIE in retrieving data of interest?*

The main contributions of this article are:

– the proposal of a transitional approach to guide table manipulation experts in exploiting LOD by relying on their abilities in data manipulation and chart creation;
– the implementation of the proposed approach in QueDI, a guided work-flow composed of 1) ELODIE, a SPARQL query builder provided on a FSI enhanced by a NL query to query LOD without explicitly using SPARQL; 2) data table manipulation and 3) chart creation.

The main *novelties* of our proposal are 1) the provision of a *querying mechanism articulated in two steps*: a SPARQL query building phase to retrieve results from LOD followed by a SQL building phase to manipulate retrieved results; 2) a *guided workflow* from data querying to knowledge representation instead of the juxtaposition of visualization mechanisms to query builders.

The rest of this article is structured as follows: in Sect. 2, we overview related work on making semantic search more usable, and we mainly focus on the trade-off between usability and expressivity they propose; in Sect. 3, we present challenges in querying LOD, the QueDI implementation overview, and a navigation scenario on DBpedia; in Sect. 4, we estimate the QueDI accuracy and expressivity by a standard benchmark dataset (QALD-9 on DBpedia) and its usability (also including temporal aspects); finally, we will conclude with some final remarks and future directions.

2   Related Work

During the past years, several different approaches have been proposed to hide the complexity of SPARQL and enable query building. Users can query KG by creating graph-like queries (such as FedViz [23], RDF Explorer [21]) or visual query formulation (e.g., OptiqueVQS [19]), they can interact with facets (e.g., SemFacet [2]), also enhanced by keyword search interfaces (such as SPARK-LIS [10] and Tabulator [5]), they can be helped by query completion (such as YASGUI [16]), users can work with summarization approaches (such as Sgvi-zler [18]), or a combination of them. The expressivity level of the querying method can be affected by the interaction model, the required usability, the efficiency. Some tools support users not only in retrieving data but also in visualizing them. We will focus on tools that combine data querying and visualization.

In Table 1, we provide an overview of the considered tools by presenting a schematic comparison of query building mode, expressivity, and the need for SPARQL awareness by users. Moreover, we also consider the provided visualization mode, and if customization and export are enabled.

Tabulator [5] leads to query (and modify) KGs without SPARQL awareness. Users can interact with an FSI where predicate/object pairs are reported for each focused element, and the user can recursively follow paths by choosing element by element. Besides the tabular representation of retrieved results, Tabulator provides basic visualizations: if results contain temporal or geographical information, the user can create timelines and/or maps. It is not mentioned if the realized visualization can be customized and/or exported.

Table 1. Comparison of interfaces to query KGs and visualize the retrieved results. For each work we report 1) the year of publication, 2) the interaction mode, expressiveness and the awareness of SPARQL for the Query builder, 3) visualization mode and the possibility to customize and export the visualization. $\sim$ means that the feature is partially covered; empty cells mean that the feature is not clarified by the author(s).

Tool	Year	Query builder			Visualization		
		Mode	Expressivity	SPARQL awareness	Mode	Custom	Export
TABULATOR [5]	2006	facet	Path Traversal	✕	time, map		
NITELIGHT [17]	2008	graph	SPARQL 1.0−	$\sim$	time, map		
VISINAV [12]	2010	facet+ keywords	BGPs	✕	time, map		✓
Sgvizler [18]	2012	text	SPARQL	✓	Google Charts	✓	
VISU [1]	2013	text	SPARQL	✓	Google Charts		
Visualbox [11]	2013	text	SPARQL	✓	chart, map, time	✓	✓
Rdf:SynopsViz [6]	2014	form	BGPs−	✕	chart, treemap, time	✕	✓
YASGUI	2017	text	SPARQL 1.1	✓	Google Charts	✓	✓
SPARKLIS [10]	2018	facet+NL	SPARQL−	✕	Google Charts + map, image	✓	✓
WQS [14]	2018	form	BGPs	✕	chart, map, time, image, graph	✓	✓
QueDI	2020	facet+NL	BGPs+	✕	chart, time, image, map	✓	✓

NITELIGHT [17] is a tool to create graphical SPARQL queries. Authors declare that it is intended for users that already have a SPARQL background since the complexity and the structures of SPARQL patterns are not masked during the query definition. A keyword browser supports the query formulation to lookup classes and properties of interest. The output of the query can be visualized as a map and/or timeline. It seems that the resulting visualization can neither be customized and exported.

VISINAV [12] leads users in looking up for a keyword of interest, without knowing the underlying data modelling. The keyword is literally searched into the KG, without extending it with synonyms and related terms. Starting from retrieved results, the user can follow paths and select facets to manipulate and extend the result set. Furthermore, VISINAV supports basic temporal and spatial visualizations. While the export seems to be provided, it is not clarified if the customization can be performed.

VISU [1] and Sgvizler [18] are both query builders and data visualization tools. Users can interact with a single or multiple SPARQL endpoints by directly using SPARQL (therefore users are SPARQL aware), manipulate the resulting table, and create customizable and exportable visualization by Google Charts. While Sgvizler is general-purpose, VISU is bound for university data.

Visualbox [11] is an environment to query KGs by SPARQL and view results by a set of visualization templates (called filters). These filters can be downloaded and wrapped in other hyper-textual documents, such as blogs or wikis.

rdf:SynopsViz [6] provides faceted browsing and filtering over classes and properties inferring statistics and hierarchies from data without requiring any further interaction by the user. Once data have been retrieved, users can visualize them by charts, treemaps, timelines according to data and needs. Visualization can be exported, but not customized by the user.

YASGUI [16] guides users in querying KGs by directly using SPARQL and visualize data through Google Charts. The query builder is enhanced by auto-completion, while the integration with Google Charts provides customizable and exportable visualizations.

SPARKLIS [10] is a query builder based on a faceted search and a natural language interface. Within the tool, it offers basic visualizations, such as maps and image viewers. Furthermore, it is integrated with YASGUI and, thus, it inherits its visualization approach. Unlike YASGUI, it can mask the complexity of SPARQL, without losing its expressiveness.

Wikidata Query Service (WQS) [14] is bound for Wikidata; it leads to the creation of queries by a form-based interface, and it provides several different visualization modes, such as charts, maps, timelines, image viewers, and graphs.

Our proposal, QueDI, is a guided workflow from KG querying to data visualization. Users can query LOD by FSI enhanced by an NL query. The interface masks an automatic and on-the-fly generation of SPARQL queries. By only considering the SPARQL query generation phase, we cover BGPs. By also considering the dataset manipulation phase, we cover aggregation and sorting. This consideration justifies that the expressivity of QueDI is more than BGP. Finally, customizable and exportable visualization can be created. Users can export the visualization as an image or as a dynamic and live component that can be embedded in any hyper-textual page, such as HTML pages, WordPress blogs and/or Wikis.

The main *difference* with the previous works is the split of the expressivity of the query building phase in an implicit creation of SPARQL queries over KGs and by direct manipulation of datasets to perform aggregation and sorting.

3   QueDI: A Guided Approach to Query and Exploit LOD

3.1   Linked Open Data Querying Challenges

The main challenges posed by querying LOD are:

- **technical complexity of SPARQL**: SPARQL is extremely expressive but writing SPARQL queries is an error-prone task, and it is largely inaccessible for lay users;
- **hard conceptualisation**: data can be modelled by domain-specific schema, or they can be domain-agnostic. Therefore, it may not be easy to conceptualize the data that users are querying;

- **heterogeneity** in data modelling: this issue is strongly related to the difficulties in conceptualization. Since different endpoints can use different vocabularies and ontologies, it is hard to figure out the terminology to use in posing questions;
- **scalability** to manage (potential) huge amount of data;
- **portability** to different endpoints;
- **readability** of queries and retrieved results;
- **intuitive use** in deriving results by few and clear clicks.

By overviewing the QueDI features and its operating mechanism, we will point our solution to these challenges.

3.2 QueDI Overview

In this section, we present the QueDI system, whose goal is to enable lay users with a background in data table manipulation to query KGs and visualize the retrieved results. To guide users in the entire workflow, we split the querying and exploitation process into three steps (Fig. 1). Each step has a clear objective, and we aim to guarantee few and clear interactions a time to provide an *intuitive use*. The implemented steps of our scaffold approach are:

Dataset creation the user starts from a SPARQL endpoint and can query the KG. This step aims to create the dataset of interest, i.e., a dataset that replies to the question of interest, without requiring any expertise in SPARQL. ELODIE implements this phase. By representing the SPARQL query results as a data table, we move from LOD to the conform zone of the experts in data manipulation. It represents the transitional approach from LOD to data table representation.

Dataset manipulation when the user is satisfied with the retrieved data, he/she can start the manipulation of the dataset to refine its information and to make it compliant with the desired visualization. In this stage, we exploit the skills of our target in data table manipulation: users can refine results, aggregate values, and sort columns. The goal of this step is to clean the data table and make it compliant with the visualization requirement.

Visualization creation (exportable and reusable) visualizations can be created and customized. This step realizes the immediate gratification for information consumers of seeing the results of their effort in a concrete artefact. We provide the customization based on the user's preferences and the export to enable the reuse also out of QueDI.

The entire workflow implemented in QueDI takes place on client-side, without any server-side computation. QueDI is released open-source on GitHub[1]. To see

---

[1] QueDI on GitHub: https://github.com/routetopa/deep2-components/tree/master/controllets/splod-controllet.

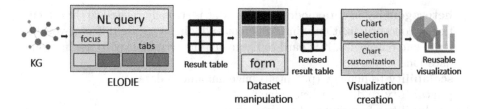

Fig. 1. It represents the QueDI guided workflow into three phases: the *SPARQL query building* implemented by ELODIE to query KGs and organize results by a tabular format; the *dataset manipulation* to refine the table and the *visualization creation* where the acquired knowledge is graphically represented.

how QueDI works, you can access to the online demo[2]. Quick tutorials[3] are available on YouTube.

ELODIE - Dataset Creation Phase. ELODIE is a SPARQL query builder provided by an FSI and enhanced by an NL query. First, the user has to select the endpoint of interest among the provided suggestions. The supported endpoints, at the moment, are DBpedia[4], also the Live version[5], the French endpoint *Persée*[6], the Italian endpoint *Beni Culturali*[7], and the Chilean endpoint *National library of Chile*[8]. By default, ELODIE will query DBpedia. Then, we can move to the querying phase.

Figure 2 represents the operating mechanism of ELODIE: the *user query* and the *focus* determine the state of the system. The NL query represents the user query, therefore herein NL query and user query will be used as synonyms. While the *user query* represents the query under construction, the *focus* represents the insertion position for applying query transformation. According to the focus, *concepts* (i.e., classes), *predicates* (i.e., relations) and resources are retrieved from the endpoint and organised in *facets* (also referred to as *tabs*). More in detail, all the sub-classes that can refine the focus are listed in the classes tab; all the predicates that have the focus as subject (direct predicates) or as the object (reverse predicates) are listed in the predicate tab.

Users can go on in the query formulation by selecting any element listed in the tabs. Therefore, the user query is iteratively defined, and the content of the queried source is discovered by inspection. It solves the problem of *conceptualised data* since users have access to valid options (referred to as *suggestions*) without explicitly asking for them. Suggestions are retrieved by path traversal queries,

---

[2] Online demo of QueDI: https://deep.routetopa.eu/deep2/COMPONENTS/controllets/splod-visualization-controllet/demo.html.

[3] YouTube tutorials of QueDI: https://youtu.be/e_o32GP-llc.

[4] https://dbpedia.org/sparql.

[5] http://live.dbpedia.org/sparql.

[6] http://data.persee.fr/sparql.

[7] http://dati.culturaitalia.it/sparql.

[8] https://datos.bcn.cl/sparql.

generic enough to be used to retrieve data from any endpoints, by solving the *portability* issue. At each query refinement, the map that models user interactions is updated by modifying the focus neighbourhood. Then, by a pre-order visit of the map, both the NL and the SPARQL queries are generated. While the NL query will be used to verbalize the user's interactions, the SPARQL query will be posed against the SPARQL endpoint to retrieve the user query's results. Once retrieved, results are organized by a tabular view. The last selected element behaves as the new focus, and, according to it, all the facets are consistently updated by querying the endpoint. This process is repeated to each user selection.

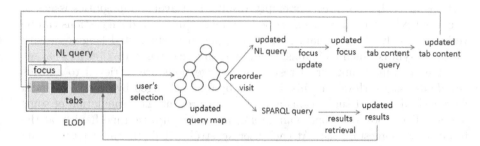

Fig. 2. *Operating mechanism of ELODIE.* Starting from a user's selection, first, the map that models the user query is updated, and then, by a pre-order visit of this tree, both the NL and the SPARQL queries are generated. When the NL query is updated, also the related box in the ELODIE interface will be updated. The focus will reflect the last added element. According to the focus, ELODIE updates the tab content by querying the SPARQL endpoint. About the SPARQL user query, when the results are retrieved, the results table is updated.

Thanks to the FSI, users are guided *step-by-step* in the query formulation. At each step, ELODIE provides a set of suggestions (concepts, predicates, operator, results) to go on in the query formulation by preventing empty results. A clarification is needed: empty results are a real desired results in a complete KG interpreted as a close world. Since common KGs are usually incomplete, empty results can be interpreted either as a real desired result or as missing information. As we can not automatically distinguish them, we prevent empty results by providing all the navigable edges outgoing from the focus as a suggestion. In other words, suggestions are focus-dependent. This exploratory search provides an *intuitive guide* in query formulation. Once a suggestion has been selected, it will be incorporated and verbalized into the current user query. It makes ELODIE a Query Builder, without asking for the SPARQL knowledge. SPARQL is completely masked to the final users by providing a solution to the *technical complexities of SPARQL*.

The query, suggestions, and results are verbalized in NL to solve the *readability* issue. Therefore, instead of showing URIs, we retrieve resources label. Class and predicate labels are obtained by looking for `rdfs:label` predicate attached to the retrieved results and by asking for the label in the user language. If these labels are missing, ELODIE looks for the English label. If also this attempt fails and resources are not attached to rdfs:label, the URL local names are exploited as labels. Suggestion labels are contextualized by phrases. For instance, instead of showing `author` as a predicate, the predicate label is wrapped into a meaningful phrase, such as `that has an author`. The user query always represents a complete and meaningful phrase. Therefore, ELODIE is a kind of NL interface. However, it is worth to notice that users cannot freely input the query, but ELODIE is provided with a *controlled* NL query used to verbalize the iteratively created user query. It makes query formulation less spontaneous and slower instead of directly writing the query in NL, but it provides intermediate results and suggestions at each step, prevents empty results, and avoids ambiguities issues of free-input NL query and out-of-scope questions. Queries and suggestions can be verbalized in English, Italian, and French, and new supported languages with the same syntax (such as Spanish) can be easily incorporated.

Only a limited number of results and suggestions are retrieved to address *scalability* issues. However, this limit can be freely changed by users. The main drawback of limited suggestions is that it can prevent the formulation of some queries. Therefore, we propose an intelligent auto-completion mechanism at the top of each suggestion list. At each user keystroke, it filters the corresponding suggestion list for immediate feedback. If the lists get empty, the list of suggestions is re-computed by asking suggestions that include the user filter.

To promote *portability*, ELODIE is entirely based on Web standards: the entire application is written in Javascript and the interface with HTML/CSS, with *zero configuration*. It only requires Cross-Origin Resource Sharing (CORS) enable SPARQL endpoint URL, i.e., a specification that enables truly open access across domain-boundaries.

As already stressed, ELODIE enables the formulation of SELECT queries (that enables the provision of results in a tabular format) by covering BGPs.

Dataset Manipulation. This phase implements a SQL query builder provided by a form-based interface. Users can *select* columns of interest, perform *aggregation, filtering, sorting*. Data manipulation is enabled by a form-based interface where users can choose the column to affect, the operation of interest (such as group by or filters), and complete it by the required parameter(s). For instance, he/she can ask for removing empty cells from a column, remove all values but numbers, filter a column by number or string operations, group the table by column values, aggregate values by counting or summing them, computing the average or detecting the minimum or maximum value. The sorting is intuitively enabled on the top of each column. These patterns enhance the BGPs of ELODIE. By aggregation we mean that users can perform `group by` and compute statistics of retrieved data, such as `count`, `average`, `sum`. By filtering, we mean that users can remove empty cells or remove cells according to textual and numeric filters, such as `contains` for strings and `less than` for numbers. By each user interaction, a SQL query is automatically created to update the result table. In this step also, the query formulation is completely masked to the user.

Visualization Creation. This step implements the exploitation phase, where users are guided in representing the acquired knowledge by charts. Besides proposing the realization of mere images, we realized a mechanism to produce dynamic artefacts that can be embedded in any blog, web page as an HTML5 component. Instead of wrapping the dataset in the chart, we embed the query to retrieve and refine the dataset in the representation. It always ensures up to date results. Therefore, if data in the queried endpoint change, also their visual representation will change as well. According to the *guidance* principle, users are provided with a vast pool of charts, such as timelines, maps, media-players, histograms, pie charts, bar charts, word clouds, treemaps. Only charts compliant with the provided data will be enabled. According to the chosen visualization mode, users can customize both the chart content and its layout. Then, the realized chart can be download as an image or as a dynamic component.

3.3 Navigation Scenario on DBpedia

We detail a navigation scenario using QueDI on DBpedia. Table 2 contains iterative queries as verbalised by QueDI of a navigation scenario that retrieves the *geographical distribution of the Italian architectural structures.* At each step, the bold part represents the last suggestion selected by the user and the underlined part represents the query focus. Suggestions can be classes (e.g., `city`), direct and inverse properties (respectively, `has a thumbnail` and `is the location`), operators (e.g., `that is equals to`) and resources (e.g., `dbr:Italy`[9]).

Fig. 3 is a collage of screenshots of the different steps of the QueDI workflow. On the top (Fig. 3.1), there is the user query at the end of its formulation by ELODIE. The focus is highlighted in yellow in the user query, and it is verbalized below the user query. When the user is satisfied with the retrieved results, he/she can move to the second step, i.e., the dataset manipulation (Fig. 3.2). In this step, we group data by city and count the architectural structures in each group. In other words, we perform data aggregation. We also sort data by the number of structures. Now, we are ready to visualize the retrieved results and represent the achieved knowledge by an exportable visual representation. The third part (Fig. 3.3) represents the geolocalized distribution of architecture structures on the Italian map.

4 Evaluation

4.1 Accuracy, Expressivity and Scalability over QALD-9

In this section, we evaluate the accuracy, expressivity, and scalability of QueDI. As stated before, we split the query formulation into two phases, i.e., a SPARQL query generation to retrieve results of interest and a SQL query generation to aggregate and sort results. Thus, we want to verify if (and in which cases) the accuracy is compromised. We hypothesize that the accuracy is affected only when

---

[9] `dbr` is the prefix corresponding to http://dbpedia.org/resource/.

the complete set of query results is so huge that the queried endpoint does not return all the results or our platform can not manage them. We want to assess the expressivity level by testing QueDI on standard benchmark for question answering and its scalability when tested against real KGs, such as DBpedia.

Table 2. *A navigation scenario in ELODIE over DBpedia.* Underlined words represent the focus, while phrases in bold represent the last selected suggestion.

Step	Query
1	Give me something
2	Give me a **city**
3	Give me a city **that is the location of** something
4	Give me a city that is the location of a **place**
5	Give me a city that is the location of a place **that is an** architectural structure
6	Give me a city that is the location of a place that is an architectural structure **that has a** lat
7	Give me a city that is the location of a place that is an architectural structure that has a lat and **that has a** long
8	Give me a city that is the location of a place that is an architectural structure that has a lat and that has a long
9	Give me a city that is the location of a place that is an architectural structure that has a lat and that has a long and **that has a** thumbnail
10	Give me a city that is the location of a place that is an architectural structure that has a lat and that has a long and that has **optionally** a thumbnail
11	Give me a city that is the location of a place that is an architectural structure that has a lat and that has a long and that has optionally a thumbnail
12	Give me a city that is the location of a place that is an architectural structure that has a lat and that has a long and that has optionally a thumbnail and **that has a** country
13	Give me a city that is the location of a place that is an architectural structure that has a lat and that has a long and that has optionally a thumbnail and that has a country **that is equals to** http://dbpedia.org/resource/Italy

Dataset. We tested QueDI, mainly focusing on ELODIE and the data manipulation phase, on the QALD-9 challenge dataset[10]. This dataset behaves as benchmarks in comparing NL Interfaces. We took into account the QALD-9 DBpedia multilingual test set[11]. For each of the 150 testing questions over DBpedia, it contains the English (among the multi-language options) verbalization of each question, the related SPARQL query, and the collection of results.

---

[10] QALD-9 challenge https://project-hobbit.eu/challenges/qald-9-challenge/.
[11] QALD-9 dataset https://github.com/ag-sc/QALD/blob/master/9/data/qald-9-test-multilingual.json.

Experiment. We evaluated the minimum number of interactions and the related needed time starting from the empty query (i.e., Give me something). Since we aim to assess the accuracy of our two-step querying approach, the expressivity of QueDI, and the scalability on real datasets and *not* the usability, we aim to minimize the exploration and thinking time required by users to conceptualize queries. Thus, we both consider the English NL formulation of the query and the related SPARQL query while performing them on QueDI. The measured time represents the best interaction time for a trained and focused user in performing questions on QueDI. In real use, interaction time will increase according to unfamiliarity with QueDI and the queried dataset and lack of focus in exploratory search. We will consider usability and interaction time in Sect. 4.2.

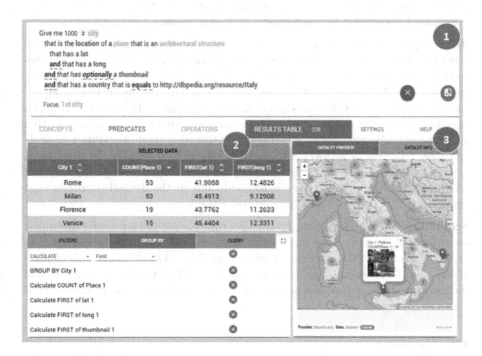

Fig. 3. The 1st component represents the user query of our navigation scenario as formalized by ELODIE to retrieve all the Italian architectural structures and related geographic information; the 2nd component represents the aggregated version of the results table to obtain the geographical distribution of the architectural structures; while the 3rd component reports the visual representations of the geographical distribution of structures on the Italian map. (Color figure online)

Results. We estimate accuracy, precision and F-measure, both for each question (*macro-measure*) and for the entire dataset (*micro-measure*). In Table 3, we report achieved results. The actual code used for the comparison and the results are provided on GitHub[12]. The challenge report [20] contains also results achieved by participants, that can be used for tool comparison.

Table 3. It reports the micro and macro precision, recall and F1 score obtained by testing QueDI on QALD-9 testing dataset.

	Precision	Recall	F1		Precision	Recall	F1
Macro results	0.75	0.95	0.83	Micro results	0.92	0.93	0.92

Expressivity. With QueDI, we can answer 143/150 questions. Not supported patterns cause the failures, i.e., make computation by SPARQL operator (3/7 cases), field correlation and not exist), and, in 2/7 cases, too many results.

Accuracy. In 20/143 cases, we both exploited ELODIE expressivity and data manipulation features. By considering the queries that requires further refinement, sorting or aggregates, we observe that: in 8/20 cases we perform a `group by` to remove duplicates; in 4/20 cases we perform `group by`, `count` as aggregation and `sort`; in 8/20 cases only sorting is required. It is worth to notice that ELODIE returns the count of table tuples without requiring any further interaction. Only one failure is caused by a too wide pool of results (*all books and their numbers of pages*) that QueDI is not able to manage. In conclusion, we can consider that by splitting the querying phase into two steps, we only lose accuracy when the desired query is too wide and/or the desired results are too much to be first collected and then refined (RQ1).

Scalability. By considering the interaction time for the 143 successful questions, we observe that: more than half of the questions (75/143) can be answered in less than 40 s (with 30 s as median and average time); 115 of them can be replied in less than 60 s (with 0,4 as average time and 0,37 as median time); only 6 of them requires a time that lies between 2 min and 3 min and a half (median time 40 s and average time 60 s).

4.2 Usability

We estimate the usability and the execution time in real use by providing a list of tasks to inexperienced participants and by collecting results of a standard questionnaire (we used SUS [13]) to assess the system *usability* (to reply to RQ2) and by comparing the needed *time* of lay users with the execution time of focused expert in accomplishing the same tasks (to reply to RQ3). Besides SUS, we also ask participants to provide *subjective* perception of the complexity and usability of QueDI, by estimating the perceived complexity in replying questions by QueDI, if the few indications provided by the training phase enable them to effectively using ELODIE, and if the effort and needed time to interact with QueDI is reasonable.

---

[12] https://github.com/mariaangelapellegrino/QueDI_evaluation.

Sampling. The users involved in the testing phase are 23 in total: 11 with skills in computer science and dataset manipulation (we involved both students still studying and already graduated) and 12 lay users, without any technical skill in querying language and heterogeneous background.

Experiment. We structured the evaluation as follows:

- we performed *15 min* of *training* to provide users with the opportunity to become familiar with QueDI (in particular with ELODIE) and the queried data by performing guided examples and by answering to queries of incremental complexity. All users were not aware of QueDI in advance;
- *testing phase*: six tasks (Table 4) are submitted in the Italian language asking for the use of DBpedia. The tasks are of incremental complexity, as for the training phase. For each task, the user reported the completion time and filled in an After Scenario Questionnaire (ASQ) using a Yes/No answers to evaluate 1) the degree of the perceived difficulty of the task by performing it through ELODIE, 2) if the time to complete the task is reasonable, 3) if the provided knowledge in the training phase is sufficient to complete the task.
- in conclusion, we asked for the fulfilment of a *final questionnaire* to evaluate i) the user satisfaction based on a Standard Usability Survey (SUS [13]) and ii) the interest in using and proposing the tool by a Behavioural Intentions (BI) survey. The questions of the BI survey are: i) *"I will use the system regularly in the future"*; ii) *"I will strongly recommend others to use the system"* and users can use a 7-point scale to reply. In the end, the participants in the evaluation study were free to suggest improvements, report the main difficulties, and the strengths of QueDI as open questions.

Table 4. Tasks provided during the evaluation of the usability of QueDI.

Task #	Query
Task 1	The Italian museums
Task 2	The games with at least 2 players
Task 3	The presenters who are the presenter of a TV Show
Task 4	The female scientists born and dead in Germany
Task 5	The athletes which are not dead
Task 6	The artists born in the same place of an athlete

Usability. The SUS score is 70 for the first group and 68 for the second one. According to the SUS score interpretation, all the values at least equal to 68 classify the system as *above the average*. That means that QueDI is considered *usable* both for technical and lay users (RQ2). In the open questions, it is clear that the perceived usability is closely related to the training phase: users - especially not experienced ones - need initial training to get familiar with KGs and their modelling. About BI, both the groups reached an average score of 5 in both the questions, i.e., there is an overall intention to reuse and propose ELODIE.

Execution time. For each group, we consider the execution time compared to the time needed to one expert of the field (also familiar with QueDI) - hence called *optimal* value. The results related to the first group - the Computer Science experts - are reported in Fig. 4a. While the results related to the second group - the lay users - are reported in Fig. 4b.

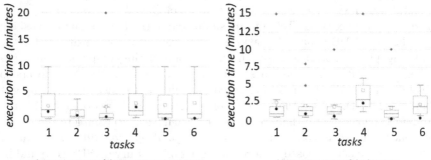

a) Execution times of the *computer science* group.   b) Execution times of the *lay users.*

Fig. 4. The time is reported on the y-axis, the tasks on the x-axis. The square icons represent the average score. The black dots represent the *optimal* value. The grey diamonds represent outliers.

In all the queries - but the last query for the second group - the minimum time needed by the participants either matches the *optimal* one or it is even better. It is a surprising result, and it means that there are users (at least one in each group) able to get familiar with QueDI and learning how to use it in a short time (RQ3). About the outliers, in the open questions, it is evident that the main difficulties are in *"finding the exact way to refer to an asked predicate or concept"* (reported by 6 out of 23 users). The participants suggest to *"insert inline help, tool-tips to help the users during the usage, examples of usage"* (reported by 9 out of 23 users). The start is considered a small obstacle to face: *"After a bit of experience, the system is pretty easy to use"* (reported by 6 out of 23 users).

5   Conclusion and Future Work

In this article, we present a transitional approach to bring closer the Semantic Web technologies and the community of tabular data manipulation and representation by enabling querying and visualization of LOD. We implement the proposed approach in QueDI, a guided workflow from data querying to their visualization by dynamic and exportable data representations. We propose to split the querying phase in SPARQL queries building and data table manipulation and we loose in accuracy only when results are too much to be first retrieved and then filtered (RQ1). The 70 score according to the SUS questionnaire reports that QueDI is considered usable by lay users (with and without table manipulation skills) (RQ2). The needed time by users with computer science background to interact with ELODIE is almost indistinguishable by the execution time of focused users, experts in QueDI features (RQ3).

Future Work. The described evaluation is a preliminary experiment to assess QueDI performance. We are defining a comparison between QueDI and state of the art. We aim to enrich the proposed endpoints by also considering the integration of a proxy to overcome the issue of not CORS-enabled endpoints. Moreover, we aim to further simplify the exploratory search in retrieving suggestions by also considering synonyms and alternative forms of the queried keywords.

References

1. Alonen, M., Kauppinen, T., Suominen, O., Hyvönen, E.: Exploring the linked university data with visualization tools. In: Cimiano, P., Fernández, M., Lopez, V., Schlobach, S., Völker, J. (eds.) ESWC 2013. LNCS, vol. 7955, pp. 204–208. Springer, Heidelberg (2013). https://doi.org/10.1007/978-3-642-41242-4_25
2. Arenas, M., Cuenca Grau, B., Kharlamov, E., Marciuska, S., Zheleznyakov, D., Jimenez-Ruiz, E.: SemFacet: semantic faceted search over yago. In: Proceedings of the 23rd International Conference on World Wide Web, pp. 123–126 (2014)
3. Bauer, F., Kaltenböck, M.: Linked Open Data: The Essentials - A Quick Start Guide for Decision Makers, vol. 710 (2011)
4. Berners-Lee, T.: 5 star open data (2012). https://5stardata.info/en/. Accessed April 2020
5. Berners-Lee, T., Hollenbach, J., Lu, K., Presbrey, J., Prud'hommeaux, E., Schraefel, M.M.C.: Tabulator redux: browsing and writing linked data. In: Proceedings of the WWW Workshop on Linked Data on the Web, LDOW (2008)
6. Bikakis, N., Skourla, M., Papastefanatos, G.: rdf:SynopsViz – a framework for hierarchical linked data visual exploration and analysis. In: Presutti, V., Blomqvist, E., Troncy, R., Sack, H., Papadakis, I., Tordai, A. (eds.) ESWC 2014. LNCS, vol. 8798, pp. 292–297. Springer, Cham (2014). https://doi.org/10.1007/978-3-319-11955-7_37
7. Damljanovic, D., Agatonovic, M., Cunningham, H.: Natural language interfaces to ontologies: combining syntactic analysis and ontology-based lookup through the user interaction. In: Aroyo, L., Antoniou, G., Hyvönen, E., ten Teije, A., Stuckenschmidt, H., Cabral, L., Tudorache, T. (eds.) ESWC 2010. LNCS, vol. 6088, pp. 106–120. Springer, Heidelberg (2010). https://doi.org/10.1007/978-3-642-13486-9_8
8. European Data Portal: Metadata Quality Assurance (2020). https://www.europeandataportal.eu/mqa/?locale=en. Accessed April 2020
9. Ferré, S.: SQUALL: the expressiveness of SPARQL 1.1 made available as a controlled natural language. Data Knowl. Eng. **94**, 163–188 (2014)
10. Ferré, S.: SPARKLIS: an expressive query builder for SPARQL endpoints with guidance in natural language. Semant. Web **8**(3), 405–418 (2017)
11. Graves, A.: Creation of visualizations based on linked data. In: Proceedings of the 3rd International Conference on Web Intelligence, Mining and Semantics, pp. 41:1–41:12 (2013)

12. Harth, A.: VISINAV: a system for visual search and navigation on web data. Semant. Web **8**(4), 348–354 (2010)

13. Lewis, J.R., Sauro, J.: The factor structure of the system usability scale. In: Kurosu, M. (ed.) HCD 2009. LNCS, vol. 5619, pp. 94–103. Springer, Heidelberg (2009). https://doi.org/10.1007/978-3-642-02806-9_12

14. Malyshev, S., Krötzsch, M., González, L., Gonsior, J., Bielefeldt, A.: Getting the most out of Wikidata: semantic technology usage in Wikipedia's knowledge graph. In: Vrandečić, D., et al. (eds.) ISWC 2018. LNCS, vol. 11137, pp. 376–394. Springer, Cham (2018). https://doi.org/10.1007/978-3-030-00668-6_23

15. Paulheim, H.: Knowledge graph refinement: a survey of approaches and evaluation methods. Semant. Web **8**, 489–508 (2016)

16. Rietveld, L., Hoekstra, R.: YASGUI: not just another SPARQL client. In: Cimiano, P., Fernández, M., Lopez, V., Schlobach, S., Völker, J. (eds.) ESWC 2013. LNCS, vol. 7955, pp. 78–86. Springer, Heidelberg (2013). https://doi.org/10.1007/978-3-642-41242-4_7

17. Russell, A.: NITELIGHT: a graphical editor for SPARQL queries. In: Proceedings of the International Conference on Posters and Demonstrations, vol. 401, pp. 110–111 (2008)

18. Skjæveland, M.G.: Sgvizler: a javascript wrapper for easy visualization of SPARQL result sets. In: Simperl, E., et al. (eds.) ESWC 2012. LNCS, vol. 7540, pp. 361–365. Springer, Heidelberg (2015). https://doi.org/10.1007/978-3-662-46641-4_27

19. Soylu, A., et al.: OptiqueVQS: a visual query system over ontologies for industry. Semant. Web **9**(5), 627–660 (2018)

20. Usbeck, R., Gusmita, R.H., Ngomo, A.N., Saleem, M.: 9th challenge on question answering over linked data (QALD-9). In: 17th ISWC, pp. 58–64 (2018)

21. Vargas, H., Aranda, C.B., Hogan, A.: RDF explorer: a visual query builder for semantic web knowledge graphs. In: Proceedings of the ISWC, pp. 229–232 (2019)

22. W3C - World Wide Web Consortium: SPARQL query language for RDF (2008). https://www.w3.org/TR/rdf-sparql-query/. Accessed April 2020

23. e Zainab, S.S., Saleem, M., Mehmood, Q., Zehra, D., Decker, S., Hasnain, A.: FedViz: a visual interface for SPARQL queries formulation and execution. In: International WS on Visualizations and User Interfaces for Ontologies and Linked Data (2015)

EcoDaLo: Federating Advertisement Targeting with Linked Data

Sven Lieber[✉], Ben De Meester, Ruben Verborgh, and Anastasia Dimou

Department of Electronics and Information Systems, Ghent University
– imec – IDLab, Technologiepark-Zwijnaarde 122, 9052 Ghent, Belgium
{sven.lieber,ben.demeester,ruben.verborgh,anastasia.dimou}@ugent.be

Abstract. A key source of revenue for the media and entertainment domain is *ad targeting*: serving advertisements to a select set of visitors based on various captured visitor traits. Compared to global media companies such as Google and Facebook that aggregate data from various sources (and the privacy concerns these aggregations bring), local companies only capture a small number of (high-quality) traits and retrieve an unbalanced small amount of revenue. To increase these local publishers' competitive advantage, they need to join forces, whilst taking the visitors' privacy concerns into account. The EcoDaLo consortium, located in Belgium and consisting of Adlogix, Pebble Media, and Roularta Media Group as founding partners, aims to combine local publishers' data without requiring these partners to share this data across the consortium. Usage of Semantic Web technologies enables a decentralized approach where federated querying allows local companies to combine their captured visitor traits, and better target visitors, without aggregating all data. To increase potential uptake, technical complexity to join this consortium is kept minimal, and established technology is used where possible. This solution was showcased in Belgium which provided the participating partners valuable insights and suggests future research challenges. Perspectives are to enlarge the consortium and provide measurable impact in ad targeting to local publishers.

Keywords: Advertisement · Federation · Linked Data

1 Introduction

Digital advertising is the act of serving advertisements ("ads") in different formats to *visitors* who consume online content on *publishers'* websites. It is a key source of revenue in media and entertainment domain: *advertisers* that set up an *ad campaign* receive revenue from the company ordering the campaign, and publishers receive money from advertisers to display ads. When setting up an ad campaign, advertisers specify which and how many ads are served (from one or more companies) as well as its format.

In *ad targeting*, an advertiser also defines a pre-selected set of visitors based on various *traits*, e.g. geography, demographics, psychographics, browsing behavior,

© The Author(s) 2020
E. Blomqvist et al. (Eds.): SEMANTiCS 2020, LNCS 12378, pp. 87–103, 2020.
https://doi.org/10.1007/978-3-030-59833-4_6

or past purchases. Ad targeting increases the probability of a visitor reacting positively compared to serving the same ad to every visitor [30], and, thus, results in higher return on investment for both publishers and advertisers.

The *profile*, the trait set of a visitor, needs to be *captured*, using *observations* via various complementary channels. For example, when Alice visits the sports page of a publisher's website more than eight times per month, that publisher – or a third-party tracker – adds the trait "liking sports" to Alice's profile (*web browsing behavior* observation). When Alice registers herself on that website and enters her birth date, her age range trait (e.g., 40–55) is also added to her profile (*demographics* observation). Alice can be targeted by the profile *"People over 35 years old liking sports"*, as her profile matches, as long as sufficient consent was provided upfront by Alice. When more traits of Alice are captured, she can be targeted by more (and more specific) ads.

However, profile data, and the revenue they entail, are unevenly distributed [3]: it was predicted that, in the first quarter of 2016, 85% of online advertising spendings would go to either Google or Facebook [14]. Such global publishers are media conglomerates and track visitors far beyond their own media properties. It is estimated that at least 68% of the most popular websites are tracked by Google [10]. These companies aggregate and centralize a large amount of data, and enable advertisers to create rich profiles. In contrast, local publishers hold only a fraction of visitor traits, as found on their own websites. Those traits are typically of higher quality compared to global companies, as local publishers have a closer relationship with their visitors. However, local publishers typically miss the opportunity to target visitors matching a requested profile, due to lack of scale, and, hence, miss out on revenue.

Combining multiple local publishers' data can improve the profiling information and make their generated profiles – due to higher quality – competitive to global publishers. However, aggregating and centralizing all data understandably comes with limitations. Recent large-scale data scandals made the general public increasingly aware of the importance of privacy and control over personal data. The introduction of the General Data Protection Regulation (GDPR) in the European Union [9] enforces explicit, freely-given consent for sharing personal data. More, sharing all data across publishers would not be well received by the publishers, as this would result in loss of competitive advantage. The data should thus remain exclusive to each publisher.

Using *federated querying* the data remains spread among – and under control of – publishers. However, it allows discovering visitors that adhere to a certain targeted profile, combining the relevant data from multiple publishers via federated querying. Linked Data [1] acts as an enabling technology: (i) the interoperable layer allows uniform and unambiguous trait descriptions across publishers and (ii) richer profiles are created via federated querying, while the data does not need to be shared across publishers. The usage of semantic technologies, thus, allows local publishers to join forces, leveling the playing field with global companies. Local publishers and advertisers do not need to fully share their data, whilst improving ad targeting.

A solution based on federated querying is devised mapping publisher's custom trait definitions to a common SKOS vocabulary [20], generating RDF datasets using RML [7] and queried using Comunica [26]. This solution is applied to and deployed in the media landscape of Flanders, Belgium, as it is explained at https://vimeo.com/374617281. A consortium was formed, dubbed *EcoDaLo*, consisting of complementary partners to deploy this interoperable layer: Adlogix, Pebble Media, and Roularta Media Group.

We present the role semantic technologies play in EcoDaLo, allowing federated advertisement targeting in Belgium. After introducing the use case (Sect. 2), we present our application (Sect. 3). Our approach was showcased by multiple companies in Belgium (Sect. 4), allowing federated integration of traits to improve targeting across local publishers. We functionally evaluate our solution (Sect. 5), present related work (Sect. 6), and conclude by discussing privacy and ethical considerations as well as key features of our solution (Sect. 7).

2   EcoDaLo

The EcoDaLo consortium is one of the first collaborations where publishers remain in exclusive control of data they collected, and a decentralized deployment is attained. Three complementary funding consortium partners participate in EcoDaLo. **AdLogix** is a development company experienced in digital advertising, which developed multiple advertising products on the international market[1]. It is responsible for providing technical support to build a production-ready system that can be used by both advertisers and publishers. **Pebble Media** is a digital sales house, representing the role of advertiser, with many partnerships in the local market[2]. **Roularta Media Group** is a multimedia group, representing the role of publisher, and market leader in the field of radio and television, magazines, and local media in Flanders[3]. As domain experts, Pebble Media and Roularta Media Group are responsible for providing technical requirements, aligned with the current advertising industry landscape. As all bases are covered by the different consortium partners, the devised solution remains in line with industrial perspectives, and chances of successful impact increases.

Motivating Example. Alice visits the websites of publishers A and B (Fig. 1). The publishers have different ways of identifying Alice's traits. Publisher A knows her age range because Alice registered her birth date: Alice is identified with id *A123* and she gets assigned trait *A_over_35* (Fig. 1, *1*). Publisher B – specialized in football content – deduces that Alice is football lover, because she visits any of the publisher's web pages more than once a week: Alice is identified with id *B456*, she gets assigned trait *B_likes_football* (Fig. 1, *2*). None of the publishers can provide enough traits to match Alice to *"sports lovers over 35"* (Fig. 1, *3*). And even if publishers could combine their user traits, it is not clear whether

---

[1] http://www.adlogix.eu/.

[2] http://www.pebblemedia.be/.

[3] https://www.roularta.be/en.

a football lover qualifies as a sports lover or not. EcoDaLo aims to enable this potential, semantically – i.e., meaningfully – combining the captured data, and serve Alice relevant advertisements, targeted at the requested profile.

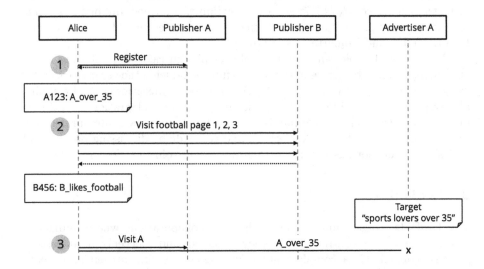

Fig. 1. Publisher A knows Alice is over 35 years old, and Publisher B that she likes football. However, Alice cannot be targeted, as her captured traits from different publishers cannot be combined.

3   Federating Advertisement Targeting with Linked Data

EcoDaLo aims to improve ad targeting by combining visitor data *across publishers*. This allows leveling the playing field between local and global publishers: local publishers can target more visitors, and their captured visitor traits are of higher quality compared to those of global publishers. Typically, integrating all publishers' data results in an additional ad server having access to a large amount of data. This provides a global fine-grained view of every individual visitor, and allows detailed analysis over all data. However, it also requires publishers to give up control over the data they captured (Fig. 2, left).

The addressed challenges include cross-publisher targeting without sharing all data and providing an extensible and scalable framework to various new partners. We chose to keep the data spread across publishers, and let a separate neutral party do federated querying on the level of captured visitor traits, using unambiguous semantic descriptions, instead of integrating all publisher's individual observations. For example, not every observation that Alice visits a football page is shared across publishers, only Publisher B's (aggregated) captured trait that Alice likes football is taken into account during federated querying. Also the aggregated captured trait is not shared with other publishers, it is only taken into account by the federated query layer.

The combination of federated querying, and only considering the captured visitor traits instead of all data, alleviates *privacy concerns*, improves *scaling behavior*, and *exploits existing infrastructure*. The disadvantage is that ad targeting by combining visitor traits is not as fine-grained as integrating all data. For example, it is not possible to target visitors that "visited at least three sports pages across all publishers in the last 10 days", as such information is not shared.

Visitors' *privacy* is protected to a certain extent: no fine-grained information is shared across consortium partners. Visitors are, to this point still, identifiable across publishers, but the captured traits (and links from these traits to unique visitors) remain under (exclusive) control of the publishers. The business rules of how those traits are captured remain exclusive to the individual publishers.

The solution *scales* as less data needs to be federated: a captured trait can be an aggregation from a large number of historical observations. Considering only the aggregations can reduce the amount of data by multiple orders of magnitude.

Publishers' *existing trait capture infrastructure* is reused, compared to installing a large new trait capture infrastructure. The existing infrastructure – optimized to aggregate large amounts of (historical) data to capture traits – remains unaltered: its output, i.e., the discovered visitor traits, serves as a data source for the federated querying. This reduces development effort for the consortium partners, and increases the chances of adoption by more publishers.

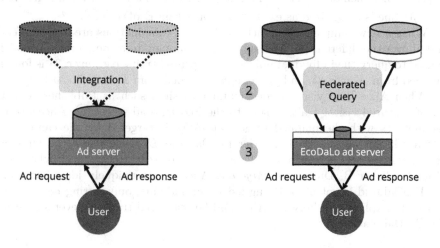

Fig. 2. Current practice (left) vs. EcoDaLo (right). Typically, all captured data is integrated in a common ad server (center-left), and publishers give up control of their data (dotted DBs, top-left). In EcoDaLo, a common ad server only captures visitor identification data (small DB, center-right). Publishers require an additional layer enabling federated querying (extra DB outlines, top-right).

In this section, we provide a high-level overview (Sect. 3.1) and an example (Sect. 3.2), after which we discuss our design considerations (Sect. 3.3).

3.1 High-Level Overview: Federated Querying with Common Identifier

Our solution consists of three main components (Fig. 2, right):

(i) The *EcoDaLo ad server* – auxiliary to the pre-existing ad servers used by each respective publisher – targets and serves ads to visitors across publishers (Fig. 2, ③). This ad server only provides the common identifier; the visitor traits remain under the individual publishers' control.

(ii) Each publisher provides a *semantic layer*, exposing the captured visitor traits mapped to an interoperable unambiguous trait model (Fig. 2, ①).

(iii) A *federated querying* intermediate layer connects the additional ad server with the individual publishers (Fig. 2, ②). Due to the explicit semantics, we provide an interoperable layer, extensible to new partners.

3.2 Example of Federated Querying with Common Identifier

Using our solution, Alice can be targeted by combining multiple traits from different publishers (Fig. 3). Alice visits a website of Publisher A as a registered visitor (Fig. 3, ①). She is identified as new visitor within EcoDaLo (EcoDaLo id *E1*, ②). Alice then browses some football pages of Publisher B as an unregistered user ③. She is recognized as existing visitor within EcoDaLo ④.

When a new campaign is launched, the trait combinations are queried, federated over the different publishers ⑤). The mapping to a common trait model is used to query the individual publisher's captured traits, e.g., *over_35* is found mapped from *A_over_35*, and *sports_lover* mapped from *B_likes_football*.

When Alice then visits a consortium publisher, such as Publisher A, her set of captured visitor traits is sent to the EcoDaLo ad server ⑥. Alice's trait set matches with the mapped target set, Alice is targeted by the campaign, and a relevant ad is served ⑦. Her EcoDaLo id *E1* makes sure the number of times Alice gets served a specific ad is monitored correctly, even when she visits Publisher B. During *ad targeting*, Alice is not uniquely identified, i.e., her EcoDaLo id is not used during federated querying, only during *ad serving*. Thus, the explicit link between Alice and her captured traits is never stored in the EcoDaLo ad server.

3.3 Design Considerations

Each publisher has its own trait definitions. This influences ad campaign definitions and visitor targeting. Before defining an ad campaign, a common, unambiguous trait model is needed for the traits targeted by advertisers, those captured by publishers, and the relationships between them. For example, Publisher A captures three age ranges ("<18", "18–35", ">35"), and Publisher B captures five age ranges ("<18", "18–25", "25–35", "35–65", ">65"): the targeted trait "over 35" is mapped differently for Publisher A and Publisher B.

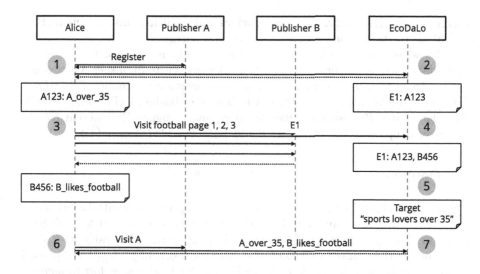

Fig. 3. Alice is targeted by combining multiple traits, from different publishers.

A semantic model further allows description of trait relations, e.g., the relationship between Publisher B's captured "likes football" and the more general "sports lover" can be specified. Instead of requiring all consortium partners to alter their system and impose usage of a common trait model, publishers map their existing captured traits to a common model. This *increases flexibility*: a single captured trait can be mapped to multiple common traits, and a combination of captured traits can be mapped to a single common trait. This increases the chances of adoption as changes in the publishers' pre-existing infrastructure and required effort are minimized.

A visitor can thus be targeted by combining the captured traits across publishers, and served a relevant ad. However, to monitor how many ads are served to how many distinct visitors, a shared identification mechanism is still needed. Multiple options were considered to identify visitor across publishers, among others, machine learning and browser fingerprinting:

Machine learning techniques could help identify individual visitors based on their combination of traits. However, more detailed data is not available – given that no fine-grained observations are shared – and this would require to create a training set of visitors and addressing the related emerging privacy concerns.

Browser fingerprints [18] provide a quasi-unique identification mechanism by combining visitors' browser and hardware traits, e.g., installed plugins, screen resolution, etc. The identification is not 100% accurate, and identification is limited to visitors using a single browser and device.

However, these options were dismissed due to the inability to provide 100% accurate results. Given the domain, where inaccuracies are already manifold (e.g., visitors using multiple devices, sharing the same accounts, etc.), the consortium decided not to add more inaccuracies. Instead, we use the EcoDaLo ad server as identifying service, which provides and explicitly links common (Eco-DaLo) ids to the visitor ids of each consortium partner.

The ad server only stores its own generated ids, mapped to the ids of the individual publishers. For example, when Alice first visits Publisher A, she is not yet identified within EcoDaLo, the ad server creates a new common EcoDaLo id *E1*, and connects this id with *A123*, Alice's id of Publisher A (Fig. 3, ②). When Alice later visits Publisher B, given her previously assigned EcoDaLo id *E1*, the ad server is updated and Publisher B's id *B456* is added (Fig. 3, ④).

4   Deployment

EcoDaLo's technical considerations include setting up the EcoDaLo ad server (Sect. 4.1), using a common trait model (Sect. 4.2), mapping each publisher's traits to that common trait model (Sect. 4.3), federating the traits (Sect. 4.4), and exposing the results to the EcoDaLo ad server (Sect. 4.5). The (development) effort for partners to integrate with the EcoDaLo set-up is kept low to increase potential uptake and growth of the consortium.

4.1   EcoDaLo Ad Server

The EcoDaLo ad server: (i) provides common visitor ids across consortium part-ners, (ii) serves ads of campaigns set up within the EcoDaLo consortium, and (iii) monitors the number of ads served to distinct visitors. As such, established pre-existing ad server software can be used to fulfill multiple requirements. We employ an ad server that provides identifiers for every visitor of any website within the consortium. Each publisher needs to modify its websites, allowing access to the EcoDaLo ad server to add these identifiers.

The expected effort is reasonable, as the publishers would need to support ads served due to campaigns set up in EcoDaLo in any case. Publishers that advertise are already required to gather GDPR-compliant visitor's consent for ad targeting involving third-parties, i.e. informing the user who will have access to which information for which purpose. Thus, no additional effort regarding the consent gathering setup is needed compared to existing solutions.

4.2   Common Trait Model

We use an interoperable, semantic model to describe the common traits, as it enables meaningful federation across publishers. We provide a Simple Knowl-edge Organization System (SKOS) taxonomy [20] based on the IAB Technology Laboratory's Audience Taxonomy 1.0[4] as common trait model. The IAB Tech-nology Laboratory (IAB Tech Lab) is an international nonprofit consortium that helps companies implement global advertising industry technical standards and solutions. We only considered IABs audience taxonomy as a possible common

---

[4] https://bit.ly/3fqVVko, hosted locally at https://bit.ly/2zfhkwe.

trait model, other trait models can be used or created instead. This taxonomy is available at http://semweb.mmlab.be/ns/iab/at_1-0, mapped from the originally published taxonomy to SKOS using YARRRML [6,15], and processed as RML rules [7,8]. The mapping rules are available at http://semweb.mmlab.be/ns/iab/mapping/iab_audience.mapping.yaml and http://semweb.mmlab.be/ns/iab/mapping/iab_audience.mapping.rml.ttl.

The modeling effort is limited compared to the typical approach where all publishers' data is integrated: only the traits need to be modeled, as opposed to all types of publisher observations and descriptions of how observations lead to a captured trait. For example, we do not need to model that the set of observations "visiting at least three football pages the last 10 days" is used to capture the "football lover"-trait. The use of a declarative mapping language allows for possibly fine-grained mappings including the use of functions but can also be created manually in a hard-coded fashion. In any case, we provide a transparent and maintainable process, adaptable for change, as the Audience Taxonomy is currently released for public comment.

4.3   Mapping to the Common Trait Model

Each publisher is required to provide a mapping of the captured internal traits to the common ones. This mapping can be many-to-many, across multiple levels. For example, "football lover" is mapped to "Sports—American Football" and the more general "Sports", and "tennis lover" is – next to "Sports—Tennis" – also mapped to "Sports". More granular mappings can be taken into account, e.g., distinguishing the levels of interest of a "football lover".

The Resource Description Framework (RDF) [5] is useful to describe the mapping, as it natively allows to unambiguously link concepts in complex relationships. For usability reasons, consortium partners – which are non-Semantic Web experts – do not need to manually write RDF triples. Instead, they provide a mapping of their custom captured traits to the common trait model, by means of a CSV file with three columns: the publisher's captured internal trait id and label, and the common trait_id from the IAB Audience Taxonomy.

This CSV file is then used to generate the RDF dataset mapping each publishers' internal traits to the common trait model. The generation description is written in YARRRML [6,15], a representation of RML [7,8] (Listing 1): the generation process remains maintainable, whilst consortium partners are not bothered with the details of how RDF triples are generated. Every time the mapping changes, i.e., when a publisher captures new visitor traits, the RDF dataset is regenerated and republished.

We provide a transparent and maintainable generation process, adaptable for change, by using RML. The generation description remains user-friendly relying on a CSV configuration document: CSV is easily handled using standard office suites, and a common export format for many software packages.

```
1   prefixes:
2       iab:   "http://semweb.mmlab.be/ns/iab/at_1-0#"
3       pubA:  "http://example.com/publisherA#"
4       ex:    "http://example.com/#"
5   mappings:
6       iabmapping:
7           sources: ["mapping.csv~csv"]
8           subject: "pubA:trait_$(id)"
9           predicateobjects:
10              - [ex:comesFrom,  "pubA:publisher~iri"]
11              - [ex:originalId, "$(id)"]
12              - [rdfs:label,    "$(label)"]
13              - [ex:iab_at,     "iab:$(trait_id)~iri"]
```

Listing 1. YARRRML file to describe the RDF generation from CSV data.

```
1   PREFIX ex: <http://example.com#>
2   PREFIX skos: <http://www.w3.org/2004/02/skos/core#>
3   CONSTRUCT {
4       ?iab    a               ex:IABSegment ;
5               rdfs:label      ?iabLabel     ;
6               ex:hasSegment   ?s            .
7       ?s      ex:hasId        ?id           ;
8               rdfs:label      ?label        ;
9               ex:from         ?fromId       .
10  } WHERE {
11      ?s      ex:iab_at       ?iab          ;
12              ex:originalId   ?id           ;
13              rdfs:label      ?label        ;
14              ex:comesFrom    ?fromId       .
15      ?iab    skos:prefLabel  ?iabLabel     .
16  }
```

Listing 2. SPARQL CONSTRUCT query for finding all captured traits across all publishers.

4.4   Federated Querying Layer

Federated querying of cross-publisher traits is enabled using the generated interoperable RDF datasets of each publisher. Each publisher's mapping dataset is generated in HDT format [11,19], and published as a Triple Pattern Fragments (TPF) endpoint [29]. The federated query engine Comunica [26] queries over the TPF endpoints of each publisher, and over the published SKOS Audience Taxonomy. An example of a federated query for all captured traits is shown in Listing 2. The traits are found across all publishers (line 11), and returned with their preferred label from the published SKOS Audience Taxonomy (line 15).

Publishing results using TPF endpoints in lower server-side CPU usage – thus requiring minimal investment of the consortium partners – and – in combination with Comunica – delivers state-of-the-art federated querying performance [29].

4.5   Developer-Friendly API

A JSON(-LD) [25] API is provided that exposes the results of federated SPARQL queries, easing integration with the EcoDaLo ad server. The JSON-LD context hides the individual URI prefixes. This API is consumed (daily) by the EcoDaLo ad server, to have an updated view of the consortium partners' captured traits.

In an initial stage, the complexities of using RDF are hidden from the partners, which lowers the threshold for new partners to join the consortium: no prior Semantic Web knowledge is needed.

5   Validation

The consortium collected focus groups to make sure the devised solution is in line with the industry's common practices. All decisions were communicated in face-to-face meetings, and feedback was gathered using the think-aloud method [24]. We discuss a launched campaign that evaluate the added benefit of EcoDaLo and compare EcoDaLo to other approaches based on six identified features.

5.1   Launched Campaign

Our devised solution reached Technology Readiness Level (TRL) 5: we implemented and validated it in a relevant environment within a launched advertisement campaign in the end of August 2019 in Flanders, Belgium.

The Belgian university Vrije Universiteit Brussel (VUB)[5] acts as client in the launched campaign and wants to target (potential) students to maximize the registrations for the open VUB day on September 7th 2019[6]. The campaign targets (combinations of) both overlapping and complementary captured visitor traits of both Roularta Media Group and Pebble Media in different advertising formats, such as "half page" or "mobile leaderboard". Additionally we measured the traffic to the website of the open day at VUB using a tracking pixel.

Our devised solution has been presented to the industrial partners and served as technological base for the described campaign. Around 1.84 million impressions were delivered by Pebble Media and 1.03 million via Roularta Media Group; VUB reported that compared to last year 300 extra people were registered for the open day. Additionally industry partners using our solution reported insights in different renumeration models, i.e. how to split revenue based on provided knowledge about visitor traits and advertising format of the impression.

5.2   Functional Comparison

To evaluate the added benefit of EcoDaLo, we perform a functional evaluation of six features, comparing EcoDaLo (*trait federation*) to the status quo of a *local publisher*, a *global publisher*, and an *integration* approach (Table 1).

Trait quality. The *trait quality* of a local publisher is – due to the locality – higher compared to those of a global publisher. This high quality is retained when integrating the captured data or federating the traits.

---

[5] https://www.vub.be/en/home.

[6] https://www.vub.be/events/2019/infodag-7-september-2019.

Table 1. Summary of functional comparison of advertisement approaches with respect to a set of identified features.

	Feature	Local publisher	Global publisher	(Data) integration	(Trait) federation
1	Trait quality	++	−	++	++
2	Scale	−	++	+	+
3	Exclusive (privacy)	++	−	−	+
4	Ease of set-up	++	++	−	+
5	Interoperability	− −	− −	−	++
6	Maintainability	−	−	−	+

Scale. The number of visitors that can be targeted, and the number of different traits that can be captured, i.e., the *scale*, increases during integration and federation, however, it does not necessarily reach the same numbers as for global publishers.

Exclusive. Captured data is shared with a global publisher or during integration: it is no longer *exclusive* to a single local publisher. During federation, only common traits are shared with the EcoDaLo ad server, the visitor's privacy with respect to all collected data is considered.

Ease of set-up. Federation requires only the mappings of aggregated traits compared to integration where all observation types must be mapped to a common model; which still requires effort but less.

Interoperability. Integration slightly improves *interoperability* by using common definitions, as compared to the closed environment of local and global publishers. However, the Linked Data principles renders the federation approach entirely interoperable and machine-understandable.

Maintainability. Attention was put into improving the *maintainability* of the federation approach, specifically, into maintainability of the common trait model generation and the trait mapping description.

6 Related Work

We describe related work regarding privacy, semantic web and advertisement.

Online behavioral advertisement (OBA) is controversial: on the one hand, it creates more relevant and efficient ads, on the other hand raises privacy concerns as it is based on personal data. For a complete overview of the topic we refer the reader to the literature review of Boerman et al. [2].

The W3C Data Privacy Vocabularies and Controls community group developed a vocabulary to annotate and categorize instances of legally compliant personal data handling [23]. This is complementary to our solution as their vocabulary describes consent and data processing purposes in EcoDaLo.

The SPECIAL project proposed a privacy-aware big data architecture focused on consent management and compliance verification [17]. It was developed in parallel with EcoDaLo. SPECIAL's sticky privacy policies, data use constraints attached to data, could be realized within EcoDaLo by also mapping consent-related information from publishers to a common data model, similar to visitor trait data, providing the added feature of ex-ante compliance checking.

Publishers join forces by introducing an integration component that allows aggregating all involved publishers' captured data [21]. This requires considerable development effort, tailored to existing publishers' data stores and detailed privacy-compliance considerations. As such, a federated approach for querying captured visitor traits is, to the best of our knowledge, novel for ad targeting.

Usage of Semantic Web technologies to enable trait federation in the media and entertainment domain was not yet investigated. Existing related work instead focuses on automatically generating meaningful targeting profiles, by (i) *classifying* content and ads to form one knowledge graph, and (ii) using that knowledge graph to improve ad *recommendation* algorithms:

The semantic *classification* is either created manually [28], or content and ads are classified automatically to a common predefined knowledge graph [4]. Choosing between manual or automatic classification typically introduces a trade-off between quality and scalability. When improving the quality of the automatic classification, existing Linked Open Data graphs are used to complete the knowledge graph [13], and the explicit semantics are exploited to provide detailed tagging of content and ads [12]. During *recommendation*, typically, graph distance metrics are used as a measure of relatedness [31], an approach applied successfully in the academic publishing domain [27].

For EcoDaLo, ad targeting profiles are created manually by the advertiser. Related work is thus complementary, enabling improvements as future work: recommendation methods can be used to suggest inclusion or exclusion of certain traits when specifying an ad campaign.

7   Conclusion

Advertising is a monetary stimulus for individuals to share their data with publishers and advertisers, in exchange for content. Although not the only option, it is very common in the media and entertainment domain. Lately, awareness rises concerning the trade-off between respecting an individual's privacy and increasing advertising revenue. In EcoDaLo, we introduce an interoperable semantic layer among local publishers allowing to exploit high-quality visitor traits using federated querying, without sharing data among consortium partners.

We conclude by discussing privacy and ethical considerations, key features of our approach as well as outlining future work.

7.1   Privacy and Ethical Considerations

The misuse of personal data, especially for discrimination, is unethical and illegal; *transparency* and *ethical guidelines* may address this issue.

Intransparency regarding the use of data collected via online behavioral advertising may be harmful and unethical if consumers are unaware [2]. The GDPR addresses transparency with respect to user-awareness about *which personal data*[7] is shared with *whom* and for which *purpose* by listing obligations regarding valid consent obtainment. Recent court rulings applied these regulations on concrete cases [16] emphasizing on explicit opt-in to give consent.

For EcoDaLo, users need to be aware which personal data of which EcoDaLo publisher is used for the purpose of online advertisement, including awareness regarding participating publishers. Users then have to explicitly give consent for this purpose, i.e. they explicitly have to opt-in. EcoDaLo assumes that publishers and advertisers act with good faith following relevant ethical guidelines [22] which goes beyond the presented technical solution.

7.2 Key Features of Our Approach

Hiding the complexities of using semantic technologies increases the potential uptake by new consortium partners. Consortium partners are not confronted with RDF triples or ontologies but, instead, rely on developer-friendly formats such as CSV and JSON. The federated querying layer and interoperable machine-understandable model are made transparent, lowering effort for consortium partners and increasing chances of enlarging the consortium. Although explicit semantics are currently hidden for consortium partners, (future) advantages are gained, compared to using an ad-hoc integration layer. Unambiguous machine-understandable trait definitions increase interoperability, and make it easier for new members to join the consortium. Reasoning can be applied to automatically enrich knowledge graph: implicit links between common traits can be discovered.

7.3 Future Work

For future work, we investigate in a complementary validation component of the federated querying which i.a. can filter results which are too narrow and could harm privacy. Also, we look into the influence of using fine-grained traits and applying more advanced queries, a.o., taking into account a captured trait's confidence level. For example, when the trait "likes sports" is captured with a low confidence level by multiple publishers, this can be combined as a single "likes sports" trait with higher confidence.

Acknowledgements. The described research activities were funded by Ghent University, imec, Flanders Innovation & Entrepreneurship (VLAIO), and the European Union. Ruben Verborgh is a postdoctoral fellow of the Research Foundation – Flanders (FWO). Special thanks to Adlogix, Pebble Media, Roularta Media Group, and Vrije Universiteit Brussel for their cooperation in EcoDaLo.

---

[7] GDPRs definition of personal data also partially overlaps with protected characteristics related to discrimination and thus ethics: https://www.equalityhumanrights.com/en/equality-act/protected-characteristics.

References

1. Bizer, C., Heath, T., Berners-Lee, T.: Linked Data - the story so far. Int. J. Semant. Web Inf. Syst. **5**(3), 205–227 (2011)
2. Boerman, S.C., Kruikemeier, S., Borgesius, F.Z.: Online behavioral advertising: a literature review and research agenda. J. Advert. **46**, 363–376 (2017)
3. Bond, S.: Google and Facebook build digital ad duopoly. Financial Times (2017)
4. Broder, A., Fontoura, M., Josifovski, V., Riedel, L.: A semantic approach to contextual advertising. In: Proceedings of the 30th Annual International ACM SIGIR Conference on Research and Development in Information Retrieval (2007)
5. Cyganiak, R., Wood, D., Lanthaler, M.: RDF 1.1 concepts and abstract syntax. Recommendation, World Wide Web Consortium (W3C) (2014). http://www.w3.org/TR/rdf11-concepts/
6. De Meester, B., Heyvaert, P., Dimou, A.: YARRRML. Unofficial draft, imec – Ghent University – IDLab (2019). https://w3id.org/yarrrml/spec
7. Dimou, A., Vander Sande, M.: RDF Mapping Language (RML). Unofficial draft, Ghent University - iMinds - Multimedia Lab (2014). http://rml.io/spec.html
8. Dimou, A., Vander Sande, M., Colpaert, P., Verborgh, R., Mannens, E., Van de Walle, R.: RML: a generic language for integrated RDF mappings of heterogeneous data. In: Proceedings of the 7th Workshop on Linked Data on the Web (2014)
9. Directorate-General for Justice and Consumers: The GDPR: New opportunities, new obligations: what every business needs to know about the EU's General Data Protection Regulation. Eu Publications, European Commission (2018)
10. Englehardt, S., Narayanan, A.: Online tracking: a 1-million-site measurement and analysis. In: Proceedings of the 2016 ACM SIGSAC Conference on Computer and Communications Security, pp. 1388–1401 (2016)
11. Fernández, J.D., Martínez-Prieto, M.A., Gutiérrez, C., Polleres, A., Arias, M.: Binary RDF representation for publication and exchange (HDT). Web Semant.: Sci. Serv. Agents World Wide Web **19**, 22–41 (2013)
12. Fernández-Canellas, D., et al.: Linking Media: adopting Semantic Technologies for multimodal media connection (2018)
13. Heitmann, B., Hayes, C.: Using linked data to build open, collaborative recommender systems. In: AAAI Spring Symposium: Linked Data Meets Artificial Intelligence (2010)
14. Herrman, J.: Media websites battle faltering ad revenue and traffic. The New York Times (2016). Stated by Brian Nowak, a Morgan Stanley analyst
15. Heyvaert, P., De Meester, B., Dimou, A., Verborgh, R.: Declarative rules for linked data generation at your fingertips!. In: Gangemi, A., et al. (eds.) ESWC 2018. LNCS, vol. 11155, pp. 213–217. Springer, Cham (2018). https://doi.org/10.1007/978-3-319-98192-5_40
16. Jabłonowska, A., Michałowicz, A.: Planet49: pre-ticked checkboxes are not sufficient to convey users consent to the storage of cookies (C-673/17 Planet49). Eur. Data Prot. Law Rev. **6**(1) (2020). https://doi.org/10.21552/edpl/2020/1/19
17. Kirrane, S., et al.: A scalable consent, transparency and compliance architecture. In: Gangemi, A., et al. (eds.) ESWC 2018. LNCS, vol. 11155, pp. 131–136. Springer, Cham (2018). https://doi.org/10.1007/978-3-319-98192-5_25
18. Laperdrix, P., Rudametkin, W., Baudry, B.: Beauty and the beast: diverting modern web browsers to build unique browser fingerprints. In: 2016 IEEE Symposium on Security and Privacy (SP) (2016)

19. Martínez-Prieto, M.A., Arias Gallego, M., Fernández, J.D.: Exchange and consumption of huge RDF data. In: Simperl, E., Cimiano, P., Polleres, A., Corcho, O., Presutti, V. (eds.) ESWC 2012. LNCS, vol. 7295, pp. 437–452. Springer, Heidelberg (2012). https://doi.org/10.1007/978-3-642-30284-8_36

20. Miles, A., Bechhofer, S.: SKOS Simple Knowledge Organization System Reference. Recommendation, World Wide Web Consortium (W3C) (2009). https://www.w3.org/TR/skos-reference/

21. Moulding, J.: Sky and Virgin prove the TV industry can set aside its rivalries to deliver the advanced ad-tech scale that buyers want. Videonet (2017)

22. Nill, A., Aalberts, R.J.: Legal and ethical challenges of online behavioral targeting in advertising. J. Curr. Issues Res. Advert. **35**, 126–146 (2014)

23. Pandit, H.J., et al.: Creating a vocabulary for data privacy. In: Panetto, H., Debruyne, C., Hepp, M., Lewis, D., Ardagna, C.A., Meersman, R. (eds.) OTM 2019. LNCS, vol. 11877, pp. 714–730. Springer, Cham (2019). https://doi.org/10.1007/978-3-030-33246-4_44

24. van Someren, M.W., Barnard, Y., Sandberg, J.: The Think Aloud Method: A Practical Guide to Modelling Cognitive Processes. Knowledge-Based Systems. Academic Press, London (1994)

25. Sporny, M., Kellogg, G., Lanthaler, M.: JSON-LD 1.0 - a JSON-based serialization for linked data. Recommendation, World Wide Web Consortium (W3C) (2014). http://www.w3.org/TR/json-ld/

26. Taelman, R., Van Herwegen, J., Vander Sande, M., Verborgh, R.: Comunica: a modular SPARQL query engine for the web. In: Vrandečić, D., et al. (eds.) ISWC 2018. LNCS, vol. 11137, pp. 239–255. Springer, Cham (2018). https://doi.org/10.1007/978-3-030-00668-6_15

27. Thanapalasingam, T., Osborne, F., Birukou, A., Motta, E.: Ontology-based recommendation of editorial products. In: Vrandečić, D., et al. (eds.) ISWC 2018. LNCS, vol. 11137, pp. 341–358. Springer, Cham (2018). https://doi.org/10.1007/978-3-030-00668-6_21

28. Thomas, E., Pan, J.Z., Taylor, S., Ren, Y., Jekjantuk, N., Zhao, Y.: Semantic advertising for web 3.0. In: Zseby, T., Savola, R., Pistore, M. (eds.) FIS 2009. LNCS, vol. 6152, pp. 96–105. Springer, Heidelberg (2010). https://doi.org/10.1007/978-3-642-14956-6_9

29. Verborgh, R., et al.: Triple Pattern Fragments: a low-cost knowledge graph interface for the Web. J. Web Semant. **37**, 184–206 (2016)

30. Wang, C., Zhang, P., Choi, R., D'Eredita, M.: Understanding consumers attitude toward advertising. In: 8th Americas Conference on Information Systems (2002)

31. Zheng, H.T., Chen, J.Y., Jiang, Y.: An ontology-based approach to Chinese semantic advertising. Inf. Sci. **216**, 138–154 (2012)

MINDS: A Translator to Embed Mathematical Expressions Inside SPARQL Queries

Damien Graux[1]([✉])(iD), Gezim Sejdiu[2](iD), Claus Stadler[3](iD),
Giulio Napolitano[4](iD), and Jens Lehmann[4,5](iD)

[1] ADAPT SFI Centre, Trinity College Dublin, Dublin, Ireland
grauxd@tcd.ie
[2] Deutsche Post DHL Group, Bonn, Germany
g.sejdiu@gmail.com
[3] Leipzig University, Leipzig, Germany
cstadler@informatik.uni-leipzig.de
[4] Fraunhofer IAIS, Sankt Augustin, Germany
giulio.napolitano@iais.fraunhofer.de
[5] Smart Data Analytics, Bonn University, Bonn, Germany
jens.lehmann@cs.uni-bonn.de

Abstract. The recent deployments of semantic web tools and the expansion of available linked datasets have given users the opportunity of building increasingly complex applications. These emerging use cases often require queries containing mathematical formulas such as euclidean distances or unit conversions. Currently, the latest SPARQL standard (version 1.1) only embeds basic math operators. Thus, to address this shortcoming, some popular SPARQL evaluators provide built-in tools to cover specific needs; however, such tools are not standard yet. To offer users a more generic solution, we propose and share MINDS, a translator of mathematical expressions into SPARQL-compliant bindings which can be understood by any evaluator. MINDS thereby facilitates the query design whenever mathematical computations are needed in a SPARQL query.

1 Introduction

During the past two decades, semantic web technologies for the web have been developed and it is now possible to produce, share, analyze and interlink large knowledge graphs (sometimes containing billions of facts) structured using the RDF W3C standard [12]. Additionally, the W3C has standardized SPARQL [14], the *de facto* query language dedicated to RDF which has been more recently improved to add new features, see *e.g.* [19] for its current version. Furthermore, several projects have been created where SPARQL public endpoints are openly available to access data such as DBpedia [9] or YAGO [16]. As a consequence, to leverage these resources the Semantic Web community has been developing more and more complex use cases involving several endpoints which are then

© The Author(s) 2020
E. Blomqvist et al. (Eds.): SEMANTiCS 2020, LNCS 12378, pp. 104–117, 2020.
https://doi.org/10.1007/978-3-030-59833-4_7

queried together using federated SPARQL queries to build or extract knowledge from combinations of multiple endpoints. In addition, these use cases sometimes require the computation of mathematical formulas which combine values according to specific patterns, to either filter or return the results. However, in the current version of the standard[1], only the four basic mathematical operators are available $(+, -, *, /)$ and some basic predefined functions, such as CEIL or FLOOR. To address this lack in the standard, some popular evaluators allow extensions to the SPARQL language to cover popular mathematical functions (*e.g.* trigonometric operations). Nonetheless, this results in queries especially built to be executed in a specific system and which therefore cannot be shared among users.

To gain in interoperability, we propose and share MINDS: a translator to embed M̲athematical expressions IN̲si̲D̲e S̲PARQL queries. Our implementation is openly available under the terms of the *Apache License version 2.0* from:

https://github.com/SmartDataAnalytics/minds

MINDS translates the given mathematical expressions into a list of SPARQL-compliant bindings *i.e.* BIND((...)AS ?var). This approach allows thereby the obtained SPARQL queries to be executed by any kind of evaluator while facilitating the task of query design.

The rest of this article is structured as follows. First, we review the related work in Sect. 2 and next, we motivate our approach with an example requiring mathematical formulas in Sect. 3. Then, we describe MINDS in Sect. 4, before presenting in Sect. 5 some accuracy results about our methods and some comparisons against existing SPARQL evaluators. In Sect. 6, we present various use cases implying the use of MINDS. Finally we conclude in Sect. 7.

2   Related Work

In this section, we provide an overview of the related work regarding mathematical formulas inside SPARQL queries. Due to the SPARQL standard lacking the specification of something essential as basic math functions[2], different approaches have emerged to serve this need.

In fact, some SPARQL evaluators do not give the possibility of computing mathematical functions inside queries at all. This is for instance the case with 4store [7], RDF3X [13] or SPARQLGX [5] which are nonetheless popular evaluators from the literature renown for their performance. However, arguably, the research focus of these systems was on optimization of joins and indexes and less on feature completeness.

Currently, all practical relevant SPARQL evaluators offer the opportunity of computing mathematical functions inside the BIND elements and projections.

---

[1] https://www.w3.org/TR/2013/REC-sparql11-query-20130321/#expressions.

[2] Currently, the *SPARQL 1.2 Community Group* which aims to advance SPARQL functionalities, is describing several mathematical operators that could be added in the next iteration of the standard. https://github.com/w3c/sparql-12/.

While the SPARQL standard defines the built-in functions as part of the syntax[3], the widely adopted approach by evaluator developers is to take advantage of the `Function Call` rule, which allows arbitrary IRIs to be used as function names. Hence, function extensions typically require no changes to the SPARQL syntax. However, the lack of standardization implies two drawbacks:

- Firstly, the namespaces, local names and signatures of functions may vary between SPARQL engines, which makes it tedious –if not prohibitive– to exchange backends.
- Secondly, the means of computation of a function and therefore the results may differ between evaluators.

All popular SPARQL evaluators –often used to serve public endpoints– such as Virtuoso [4], Jena-Fuseki [8], GraphDB[4] and Stardog[5] feature mathematical functions, yet, using different IRIs. For instance, Virtuoso uses the `bif:` namespace, whereas Stardog reuses the XPath function namespace[6]. Using such an approach of naming differently similar function/operator[7] implies a loss of interoperability, especially, it make the design of federated SPARQL queries far more complex. Finally, some evaluators implement GeoSPARQL [2] giving then access to spatial functions for use in SPARQL queries such as finding a distance or computing a convex hull.

Compared with existing evaluators which provide sometimes built-in mathematical functions, MINDS chooses to use approximations when necessary in order to remain fully compliant with the SPARQL language.

3   Motivating Example

To have a better understanding of when mathematics may be needed in SPARQL queries, we consider a use case based on the geographical position of fossils found. Having a dataset recording the found fossils, we want to list the fossils:

a. found in the last ten years;
b. located 100 km around a specific position;
c. older than 1 000 years.

For clarity reasons, we will consider a simplified dataset recording Cartesian positions, a ^{14}C-ratio and the discovery year. Each fossil is then represented by an identifier using the following structure:

---

[3] https://www.w3.org/TR/sparql11-query/#grammar.

[4] https://ontotext.com/products/graphdb/.

[5] https://www.stardog.com/.

[6] https://www.w3.org/2005/xpath-functions/math#.

[7] Implementations for built-in STDEV in Virtuoso, Fuseki, Stardog, Sesame: https://gist.github.com/albertmeronyo/c6ab285d0b73b05392e2f9b8a5bbea82.

```
:fossilId   :type       :fossil .
:fossilId   :abscissa   "XXX"   .
:fossilId   :ordinate   "YYY"   .
:fossilId   :foundIn    "year"  .
:fossilId   :c14rate    "ratio" .
```

As a consequence, to list all the fossils, one might run this SPARQL query: SELECT ?f WHERE { ?f :type :fossil}. In the rest of this Section, we will refine step by step this query to add the restrictions specified above, emulating the process of a query designer.

a – Found in the last ten years. This constraint implies the filtering of the records according to the year of their discovery. Considering that the current year is 2020, we will keep only fossils found after 2010 and we can ask:

```
SELECT ?f WHERE {
    ?f :type     :fossil .
    ?f :foundIn ?Y        .
    FILTER( (2020-?Y) <= 10 ) }
```

In this particular case, only a simple FILTER (involving a simple operation) is required to refine the join.

b – 100 km around a position. Then, we want to return fossils found around a specific position whose Cartesian coordinates are (Px,Py). To do so, we have to compute Euclidean distances between this position and the fossils using the classic formula: $d = \sqrt{\Delta x^2 + \Delta y^2}$. However, according to the standard, there is no square operator and no square-root. Obviously, we can escape from these issues easily by comparing d^2 instead of d. Our SPARQL query thus becomes:

```
SELECT ?f WHERE {
    ?f :type     :fossil .
    ?f :foundIn   ?Y      .
    ?f :abscissa ?x       .
    ?f :ordinate ?y       .
    FILTER( (2020-?Y) <= 10 )
    FILTER( ( (?x-Px)*(?x-Px) + (?y-Py)*(?y-Py) ) <= 100*100 ) }
```

As one can see, the FILTER condition is getting longer –increasing the probability of errors and typos for example– and in this example we only deal with simplified data (for instance no unit conversions are needed).

c – Older than 1 000 years. The last condition only retains fossils which are older than 1 000 years. However, the considered dataset does not share ages but instead ^{14}C-ratios r of fossils which can be used using radiocarbon dating – considering the ^{14}C half-life $t_{1/2}$ *i.e* 5 700 years– to find the age $t(r)$ according to the following formula:

$$t(r) = \left(\frac{\ln(r)}{-0.693} \right) \cdot t_{1/2}$$

This expression involves the natural logarithm which is, however, not part of the standard. Therefore, to compute this expression, the query designer has to approximate the logarithm, using for example a decomposition in series:

$$\forall y \in]0, +\infty[, \ \ln(y) = 2 \sum_{k=0}^{+\infty} \frac{1}{2k+1} \left(\frac{y-1}{y+1}\right)^{2k+1}$$

The FILTER can now by written: FILTER(5700*?LOG/(-0.693)<=1000) where ?LOG is a variable embedding the logarithm approximation whose result quality depends on the number of terms used in the decomposition. Considering only the first three terms ($k \in [0,2]$) and the ^{14}C-ratio ?rate of fossils, we have:

```
BIND(( (?rate-1)/(?rate+1) ) AS ?z )
BIND(( ?z ) AS ?t0 )
BIND(( (1/3)*(?z*?z*?z) ) AS ?t1 )
BIND(( (1/5)*(?z*?z*?z*?z*?z)) AS ?t2 )
BIND(( 2*(?t0 + ?t1 + ?t2) ) AS ?LOG )
FILTER(5700*?LOG/(-0.693)<=1000)
```

As a consequence, it appears that building this simple approximation for its first three terms already leads to a rather complicated query.

Furthermore. As stated previously, the example has been simplified for the sake of clarity. Firstly, the series approximation should indeed involve more terms *i.e.* at least 5 (see Sect. 5 for more details about the approximation preciseness). Secondly, when dealing with geographical data on Earth, latitude and longitude coordinates are actually preferred to Cartesian ones. Thus, considering two points $P_1(lat_1, lon_1)$ and $P_2(lat_2, lon_2)$, the distance d should be calculated using the Haversine formula to calculate the great-circle distance:

$$a = \sin^2\left(\frac{\Delta\varphi}{2}\right) + \cos\varphi_1 . \cos\varphi_2 . \sin^2\left(\frac{\Delta\lambda}{2}\right)$$
$$c = 2 \ . \ \mathrm{atan2}\left(\sqrt{a}, \sqrt{1-a}\right) \quad , \text{and} \begin{cases} \varphi & \text{latitude in rad:} \ \frac{lat.\pi}{180} \\ \lambda & \text{longitude in rad:} \ \frac{lon.\pi}{180} \\ R & \text{the Earth radius: } 6\,371 \text{ km} \end{cases}$$
$$d = R \ . \ c$$

Thereby, to compute d with this formula, several non-standard functions are required: **7** trigonometric ones and **2** square-roots. If this very query were to be evaluated, the designer would have to write herself the multiple decompositions in series which would be tedious and a possible source of errors. In the next Section, we introduce MINDS: our solution to help query designers when dealing with mathematical expressions.

4   MINDS: From a Math Formula to SPARQL Bindings

To tackle this gap in the SPARQL standard, and to help query designers in their tasks, we developed a software called **MINDS**. In a nutshell, it allows users to input a mathematical expression and obtain –only using standard operators and keywords– the exact corresponding translation, or an approximation if a decomposition in series has to be involved.

```
Expression = Expression BinOp Expression
           | Expression ** [:digit:]
           | LeftOp Expression
           | BiParamOp Expression , Expression
           | ( Expression )
           | ?[:Alphanum:]
           | [:digit:].[:digit:]
     BinOp = + | - | * | /
    LeftOp = ln | exp | sqrt
           | sin | cos | tan
           | -
 BiParamOp = atan2
```

Fig. 1. Grammar of the expressions understood by MINDS.

Practically, we developed MINDS as an external software which can be run when designing queries. It is written in Python [18] and its core currently represents about 500 lines of code. Technically, the given formula is parsed using a dedicated implementation of the popular Lex and Yacc tools [11] for Python named PLY[8]. Then, once the formula is split into tokens, the translating rules are applied recursively to generate the final result. For instance, considering again the example of Sect. 3, the "2020-?Y" expression will be translated into:

```
#math2sparql > 2020-?Y
BIND ( ( FLOOR((2020-xsd:double(?Y))*100)/100 ) AS ?result )
```

Compared to the solution presented in Sect. 3, the actual binding is already more complicated: first, since it specifies that ?Y should be considered as a double; and second, since it truncates the result to keep only two digits of precision with the FLOOR keyword of the standard. Actually, this precision parameter can be set by the user in MINDS, for instance to 5:

```
#math2sparql > precision = 5
#math2sparql > 2020-?Y
BIND ( ( FLOOR((2020-xsd:double(?Y))*100000)/100000 ) AS ?result )
```

Therefore, MINDS is still relevant to handle even simple expressions that are cumbersome to express in SPARQL such as the d^2 (*i.e.* a squared Euclidean distance) of the previous Section:

```
#math2sparql > (?x-?Px)**2 + (?y-?Py)**2
BIND ( ( FLOOR((
(1*(xsd:double(?x)-xsd:double(?Px))*(xsd:double(?x)-xsd:double(?Px)))+
(1*(xsd:double(?y)-xsd:double(?Py))*(xsd:double(?y)-xsd:double(?Py)))
)*100)/100 ) AS ?result )
```

---

[8] Python Lex-Yacc repository: https://github.com/dabeaz/ply.

$$\exp x = \sum_{k=0}^{+\infty} \frac{x^k}{k!}$$

$$\sin x = \sum_{k=0}^{+\infty} (-1)^k \frac{x^{2k+1}}{(2k+1)!}$$

$$\ln x = 2.\sum_{k=0}^{+\infty} \frac{1}{2k+1} \left(\frac{x-1}{x+1}\right)^{2k+1}$$

$$\cos x = \sum_{k=0}^{+\infty} (-1)^k \frac{x^{2k}}{(2k)!}$$

$$\sqrt{x} = \sum_{k=0}^{+\infty} \frac{1}{k!} \left(\sum_{t=0}^{+\infty} \frac{1}{2t+1} \left(\frac{x-1}{x+1}\right)^{2t+1}\right)^k$$

$$\tan x = \frac{\sin x}{\cos x}$$

$$\mathrm{atan2}(y,x) = 2.\arctan \frac{y}{\sqrt{x^2+y^2}+x}$$

$$\arctan x = \sum_{k=0}^{+\infty} (-1)^k \frac{x^{2k+1}}{2k+1}$$

Fig. 2. Series currently used by MINDS.

We furthermore describe in Fig. 1 the grammar which is understood by MINDS. In particular, our translator is able to deal with the four basic operators of SPARQL (*i.e.* + - * /) extended with the power operator (** in MINDS) while respecting conventional priorities. Moreover, our solution also provides several translation rules to deal with mathematical functions *e.g.* trigonometric functions and even with functions of multiple variables *e.g.* atan2. Nonetheless, these additional functions are not part of the standard and have to be expressed only using allowed SPARQL operators: MINDS is then able to compute approximations to translate into bindings these functions. Indeed, it uses when necessary a series decomposition such as the ones listed in Fig. 2 and technically a new binding is generated for each series so that the query evaluator might be able to store the sub-result. For instance, considering $x^2 + \exp(y + 3z)$ which involved the computation of the exponential of a linear expression, MINDS returns:

```
#math2sparql > ?X**2 + exp (?Y + 3 * ?Z)
BIND ((0+(1)/1.0                                      # 1
  +(1*(xsd:double(?Y)+3*xsd:double(?Z)))/1.0   # y + 3z
  +(1*(xsd:double(?Y)+3*xsd:double(?Z))
     *(xsd:double(?Y)+3*xsd:double(?Z)))/2.0   # (y+3z)²/2!
  +(1*(xsd:double(?Y)+3*xsd:double(?Z))
     *(xsd:double(?Y)+3*xsd:double(?Z))
     *(xsd:double(?Y)+3*xsd:double(?Z)))/6.0   # (y+3z)³/3!
  +(1*(xsd:double(?Y)+3*xsd:double(?Z))
     *(xsd:double(?Y)+3*xsd:double(?Z))
     *(xsd:double(?Y)+3*xsd:double(?Z))
     *(xsd:double(?Y)+3*xsd:double(?Z)))/24.0  # (y+3z)⁴/4!
)AS ?sub1)
BIND ( ( FLOOR((
    (1*xsd:double(?X)*xsd:double(?X)) +?sub1   # x² + sub₁
  )*100)/100 ) AS ?result )
```

As expected, MINDS automatically converts the exponential part into an approximation using the classic series of the exponential (see Fig. 2 for more

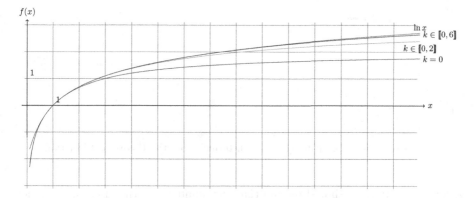

Fig. 3. Natural logarithm and its approximations.

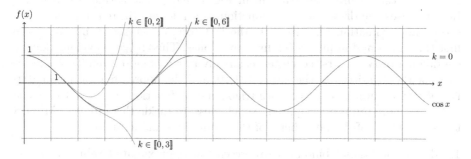

Fig. 4. Cosine and its approximations.

details); in this case only the first five terms of the series where considered. As it will be described in Sect. 5, the more terms are involved the more precise the results will be; nonetheless, it is also important to mention that MINDS allows query designers to choose as a parameter this number of terms. Moreover, it is able to understand any kind of combination using its recognized keywords and it generates recursively the sub-bindings when necessary.

5   Precision Results

First of all, we want to pinpoint that the bindings generated by MINDS offer the same orders of magnitude as the tested built-in functions in terms of execution times. Indeed, the evaluation of a `BIND` expression or the call to an internal method are both executed in sub-second times; for more details, we refer the reader to the end of this Section, where external links of running queries on various SPARQL endpoints are available.

Moreover, since MINDS uses approximations based on series for some mathematical functions (see Fig. 2 for details), we further describe in this Section the accuracy of such a method before comparing MINDS with built-in functions of popular SPARQL endpoints.

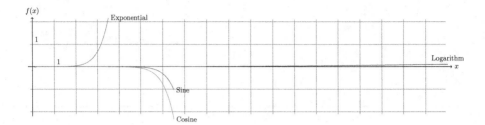

Fig. 5. Approximation drifts (first seven terms) from the theoretical functions.

Accuracy. First, we should remind that the number of terms used in the series has an impact on the quality of the approximation. Here, we review the approximation of the natural logarithm ln in Fig. 3, and of the cosine cos in Fig. 4. In both cases, we draw the exact function as a reference in red, together with several approximations: in blue only the first term of the series, in orange the first three ones and in purple the first seven ones. Thereby, it is evident that by considering **only** the first seven terms already provides more than 95% of accuracy for the logarithm in the interval [1,20] and the approximation for ln(100) is still 80% accurate. However, with trigonometric functions (see *e.g.* the cosine in Fig. 4), more terms are required. Nonetheless, to tackle this problem, MINDS takes advantage of the periodicity of these functions and actually:

1. adds an additional binding to represent an approximated value of 2π *i.e.* BIND((6.28318530718) AS ?2P);
2. replaces the expression ?f inside the sin or the cos function with the remainder of the division of ?f by 2π *i.e.* (?f - ?2P * FLOOR(?f/?2P)).

This method allows MINDS to stay within an interval in which the accuracy remains above 80% with the first seven terms. More generally, in Fig. 5, we present the drifts between mathematical functions and their respective approximations using the first seven terms of their series. This representation allows the query designers to determine the intervals where the proposed approximations of MINDS still have an accuracy above a chosen threshold, letting them decide the appropriate number of terms in the series to be generated.

Comparison with Built-in Functions. Since mathematical functions are not part of the SPARQL standard [19], most of the popular systems providing endpoints have implemented their own versions of some functions (see Sect. 2 for more details about these systems). In this study, we also present comparisons between MINDS approximations and the built-in functions from some of these systems, namely: Virtuoso[9] [4], GraphDB[10] and JenaFuseki[11] [8].

---

[9] https://virtuoso.openlinksw.com/.
[10] https://ontotext.com/products/graphdb/.
[11] https://jena.apache.org/documentation/fuseki2/.

```
SELECT * WHERE {
  VALUES ?V { 0.1 0.2 0.5 1 2 3 4 5 6 7 8 9 10 20 50 100 }
  BIND (( (?V-1)/(?V--1.) ) AS ?ratio)
  BIND (( bif:log(?V) ) AS ?BuiltInLog )
  BIND (( 2*?ratio ) AS ?OneTerm )
  BIND (( 2*( ?ratio --
           (1/3.)*?ratio*?ratio*?ratio--
           (1/5.)*?ratio*?ratio*?ratio*?ratio*?ratio )
       ) as ?ThreeTerms )
  BIND (( 2*( ?ratio --
           (1/3.)*?ratio*?ratio*?ratio--
           (1/5.)*?ratio*?ratio*?ratio*?ratio*?ratio--
           (1/7.)*?ratio*?ratio*?ratio*?ratio*?ratio*?ratio*?ratio--
           (1/9.)*?ratio*?ratio*?ratio*?ratio*?ratio*?ratio*?ratio*?ratio*?ratio--
           (1/11.)*?ratio*?ratio*?ratio*?ratio*?ratio*?ratio*?ratio*?ratio*
                   ?ratio*?ratio--
           (1/13.)*?ratio*?ratio*?ratio*?ratio*?ratio*?ratio*?ratio*?ratio*
                   ?ratio*?ratio*?ratio*?ratio )
       ) as ?SevenTerms )
}
```

Fig. 6. Query involving Virtuoso's built-in *ln* and approximations for different values.

In Table 1, we present the raw results of a SPARQL query which computes on Virtuoso for several values (?V): the built-in natural logarithm (?BuilInLog) using the bif: prefix and three bindings generated by MINDS varying the number of terms involved *i.e.* one, three and seven (see Fig. 6). We observe that the accuracy measured corresponds to the one expected theoretically (as drawn *e.g.* in Fig. 3 and 4). This observation implies that the Virtuoso engine executes exactly the operations listed in the bindings (without rounding nor truncating).

More generally, since the built-in functions are specific addons provided by the systems, the set of available mathematical functions may vary across them: for instance, GraphDB provides very specific functions such as "$hypot(x, y)$" which returns $\sqrt{x^2 + y^2}$ or "$IEEEremainder(x, y)$" which is the remainder operation on two arguments as prescribed by the IEEE 754 standard. Furthermore, currently (without MINDS), the query designers have to tune their SPARQL queries for each evaluation engine. For example, we list here various syntaxes to evaluate a logarithm:

```
# Virtuoso.
SELECT * WHERE { BIND ((bif:log(1234))AS ?log) }
```

```
# GraphDB.
PREFIX f: <http://www.ontotext.com/sparql/functions/>
SELECT * WHERE { BIND ((f:log(1234))AS ?log) }
```

```
# Fuseki2.
PREFIX math: <http://www.w3.org/2005/xpath-functions/math#>
SELECT * WHERE { BIND ((math:log(1234))AS ?log) }
```

Table 1. Virtuoso's built-in natural logarithm vs some MINDS bindings.

?V	?BuiltInLog	?OneTerm	?ThreeTerms	?SevenTerms
0.1	−2.30259	−1.636363636363636	−2.148161762423083	−2.28612550677627
0.2	−1.60944	−1.333333333333333	−1.583539094650206	−1.608934294900188
0.5	−0.693147	−0.666666666666667	−0.693004115226337	−0.693147170256012
1	0.0	0	0	0
2	0.693147	0.666666666666667	0.693004115226337	0.693147170256012
3	1.09861	1	1.095833333333333	1.098607062425422
4	1.38629	1.2	1.375104	1.386202224193573
5	1.60944	1.333333333333333	1.583539094650206	1.608934294900188
6	1.79176	1.428571428571429	1.745899525991154	1.790187408711124
7	1.94591	1.5	1.876171875	1.942329693525345
8	2.07944	1.555555555555556	1.983078460261816	2.072740626022152
9	2.19722	1.6	2.072405333333333	2.186225968329208
10	2.30259	1.636363636363636	2.148161762423083	2.28612550677627
20	2.99573	1.80952380952381	2.545790028209391	2.880218635963087
50	3.91202	1.92156862745098	2.840323022038755	3.419833927257202
100	4.60517	1.96039603960396	2.950171566927436	3.64870669515376

Notice that it is possible to directly run these examples –based on the natural logarithm[12]– on several systems, considering that these systems are used to provide public SPARQL endpoints by a number of popular services, some of which available at the following links:

- **Virtuoso** on the DBpedia endpoint ⌁;
- **GraphDB** on the FactForge endpoint ⌁;
- **Fuseki2** on the ZBW Labs endpoint ⌁.

The three above hypertext links provides visualizations of the SPARQL queries and automatically compute and display the results. They provide similar results as the ones already presented in Table 1.

6 Use Cases

MINDSaims to be a generic tool which can be integrated into existing system for SPARQL parsing or mapping to different transformations. To this aim we are developing a number of use case implementations on different tools and systems. We group such use cases into two different categories:

Integration
SPARQL–to–SQL rewriter – Sparqlify. Sparqlify[13] is a SPARQL-SQL rewriter that enables the definition of RDF views on relational databases and their

---

[12] More examples online from https://smartdataanalytics.github.io/minds/ where some other built-in functions are reviewed with other sets of values.

[13] https://github.com/SmartDataAnalytics/Sparqlify.

querying using SPARQL [15]. MINDSis being used for mathematical transformations into SPARQL bindings embedded into Sparqlify. Users will write SPARQL queries following the instructions represented by MINDSand then Sparqlify will take over the query rewriter into SQL syntax.

Semantic Analytics Stack – SANSA. SANSA [10] is an open source[14] *data flow processing engine* for performing distributed computation over large-scale RDF datasets. It provides data distribution, communication, and fault tolerance for manipulating massive RDF graphs and applying machine learning algorithms on the data at scale. SANSA uses Sparqlify as an underlying infrastructure for the integration of existing SPARQL-to-SQL rewriting tools. By doing so, it enables mathematical transformations as well via MINDSas a support add-on.

Usability

Blockchain – Alethio Use Case. Alethio[15] is modeling an Ethereum analytics platform that endeavors to provide transparency over the transaction pool of the Ethereum network. Their 5 billion triple dataset contains large scale blockchain transaction data modelled as RDF according to the structure of the Ethereum ontology[16]. Alethio has been using SANSA as a scalable processing engine for their large-scale data processing tasks, such as querying the data in real time via SPARQL and performing related analytics [6,17]. MINDS was used through SANSA integration and served as an easy-to-use mathematical function evaluator, such as time-series of the latest exchange values, average transaction size or even filtering some chains considering geometrical-mean of some included parameters.

Geospatial Data – SLIPO. SLIPO[17] was an EU Horizon2020 project which aimed at developing linked data technologies for the scalable and quality-assured integration of Big Point of Interest (POI) datasets [1]. SLIPO used SANSA as a scalable querying engine to deal with their large-scale POIs data [3]. In particular, SLIPO aimed at discovering areas of interests using POI datasets which implies, for instance, searching road segments where amenities with some common parameters are located. To do so, MINDS is being used there to filter POIs which are inside a convex hull.

7 Conclusion

In this article we introduced MINDS[18], a translator of mathematical expressions into SPARQL bindings. MINDS is also open source and shared on the Github platform which, in addition, provides us with the needed tools to manage an

---

[14] https://github.com/SANSA-Stack.

[15] https://aleth.io/.

[16] https://github.com/ConsenSys/EthOn.

[17] http://www.slipo.eu/.

[18] MINDS web-page: https://smartdataanalytics.github.io/minds/ which offers more information and details about the software such as for instance tutorials, running examples inside other SPARQL evaluators, accuracy charts.

open-source software *i.e.* a bug tracker, a way to integrate external contributions or also a release generator. We do hope this tool will help query designers in their tasks by providing *in an instant* the SPARQL compliant translation of complicated mathematical expressions, while giving them the ability of adjusting parameters in approximations.

Acknowledgments. This research was conducted with the financial support of the European Union's Horizon 2020 research and innovation programme under the Marie Skłodowska-Curie under Grant Agreement No. 801522 at the ADAPT SFI Research Centre at Trinity College Dublin. The ADAPT SFI Centre for Digital Media Technology is funded by Science Foundation Ireland through the SFI Research Centres Programme and is co-funded under the European Regional Development Fund (ERDF) through Grant #13/RC/2106.

References

1. Athanasiou, S., Giannopoulos, G., Graux, D., Karagiannakis, N., Lehmann, J., Ngomo, A.C.N., Patroumpas, K., Sherif, M.A., Skoutas, D.: Big POI data integration with linked data technologies. In: EDBT, pp. 477–488 (2019)
2. Battle, R., Kolas, D.: Geosparql: Enabling a geospatial semantic web. Semant. Web J. **3**(4), 355–370 (2011)
3. Dadwal, R., Graux, D., Sejdiu, G., Jabeen, H., Lehmann, J.: Clustering pipelines of large RDF POI data. In: Hitzler, P., Kirrane, S., Hartig, O., de Boer, V., Vidal, M.-E., Maleshkova, M., Schlobach, S., Hammar, K., Lasierra, N., Stadtmüller, S., Hose, K., Verborgh, R. (eds.) ESWC 2019. LNCS, vol. 11762, pp. 24–27. Springer, Cham (2019). https://doi.org/10.1007/978-3-030-32327-1_5
4. Erling, O., Mikhailov, I.: RDF support in the virtuoso DBMS. In: Networked Knowledge-Networked Media, pp. 7–24. Springer, Berlin (2009)
5. Graux, D., Jachiet, L., Genevès, P., Layaïda, N.: SPARQLGX: Efficient distributed evaluation of SPARQL with apache spark. In: Groth, P., Simperl, E., Gray, A., Sabou, M., Krötzsch, M., Lecue, F., Flöck, F., Gil, Y. (eds.) ISWC 2016. LNCS, vol. 9982, pp. 80–87. Springer, Cham (2016). https://doi.org/10.1007/978-3-319-46547-0_9
6. Graux, D., Sejdiu, G., Jabeen, H., Lehmann, J., Sui, D., Muhs, D., Pfeffer, J.: Profiting from kitties on Ethereum: Leveraging blockchain RDF data with SANSA. In: SEMANTiCS Conference (2018)
7. Harris, S., Lamb, N., Shadbolt, N.: 4store: The design and implementation of a clustered RDF store. In: 5th International Workshop on Scalable Semantic Web Knowledge Base Systems (SSWS2009), pp. 94–109 (2009)
8. Jena, A.: Apache jena fuseki. The Apache Software Foundation (2014)
9. Lehmann, J., Isele, R., Jakob, M., Jentzsch, A., Kontokostas, D., Mendes, P.N., Hellmann, S., Morsey, M., van Kleef, P., Auer, S., Bizer, C.: DBpedia - A large-scale, multilingual knowledge base extracted from wikipedia. Semant. Web J. **6**(2), 167–195 (2015). http://jens-lehmann.org/files/2014/swj_dbpedia.pdf
10. Lehmann, J., Sejdiu, G., Bühmann, L., Westphal, P., Stadler, C., Ermilov, I., Bin, S., Chakraborty, N., Saleem, M., Ngonga, A.C.N., Jabeen, H.: Distributed semantic analytics using the SANSA stack. In: Proceedings of 16th International Semantic Web Conference - Resources Track (ISWC'2017) (2017). http://svn.aksw.org/papers/2017/ISWC_SANSA_SoftwareFramework/public.pdf

11. Levine, J.R., Mason, T., Brown, D.: Lex & Yacc. O'Reilly Media, Inc (1992)
12. Manola, F., Miller, E., McBride, B., et al.: RDF primer. W3C Recommendation 10(1–107), 6 (2004)
13. Neumann, T., Weikum, G.: The RDF-3X engine for scalable management of RDF data. VLDB J. Int. J. Very Large Data Bases 19(1), 91–113 (2010)
14. Prud'Hommeaux, E., Seaborne, A., et al.: SPARQL query language for RDF. W3C Recommendation 15 (2008). www.w3.org/TR/rdf-sparql-query/
15. Stadler, C., Sejdiu, G., Graux, D., Lehmann, J.: Sparklify: A scalable software component for efficient evaluation of SPARQL queries over distributed RDF datasets. In: Ghidini, C., Hartig, O., Maleshkova, M., Svátek, V., Cruz, I., Hogan, A., Song, J., Lefrançois, M., Gandon, F. (eds.) ISWC 2019. LNCS, vol. 11779, pp. 293–308. Springer, Cham (2019). https://doi.org/10.1007/978-3-030-30796-7_19
16. Suchanek, F.M., Kasneci, G., Weikum, G.: Yago: A core of semantic knowledge. In: Proceedings of the 16th International Conference on World Wide Web, WWW 2007, pp. 697–706. ACM, New York (2007). https://doi.org/10.1145/1242572.1242667
17. Sui, D., Sejdiu, G., Graux, D., Lehmann, J.: The hubs and authorities transaction network analysis using the SANSA framework. In: SEMANTiCS Conference (2019)
18. Van Rossum, G., Drake, F.L.: Python Language Reference Manual. Network Theory, Bristol (2003)
19. W3C SPARQL Working Group, et al.: SPARQL 1.1 overview (2013). http://www.w3.org/TR/sparql11-overview/

Integrating Historical Person Registers as Linked Open Data in the WarSampo Knowledge Graph

Mikko Koho[1,2(✉)], Petri Leskinen[1], and Eero Hyvönen[1,2]

[1] Semantic Computing Research Group (SeCo), Aalto University, Espoo, Finland
[2] HELDIG – Helsinki Centre for Digital Humanities, University of Helsinki, Helsinki, Finland
mikko.koho@helsinki.fi

Abstract. Semantic data integration from heterogeneous, distributed data silos enables Digital Humanities research and application development employing a larger, mutually enriched and interlinked knowledge graph. However, data integration is challenging, involving aligning the data models and reconciling the concepts and named entities, such as persons and places. This paper presents a record linkage process to reconcile person references in different military historical person registers with structured metadata. The information about persons is aggregated into a single knowledge graph. The process was applied to reconcile three person registers of the popular semantic portal "WarSampo – Finnish World War 2 on the Semantic Web". The registers contain detailed information about some 100 000 people and are individually maintained by domain experts. Thus, the integration process needs to be automatic and adaptable to changes in the registers. An evaluation of the record linkage results is promising and provides some insight into military person register reconciliation in general.

1 Introduction

A way to enhance our understanding about history is to integrate data from complementary information sources in an interoperable way. In *record linkage (RL)* [2,6,13], the goal is to find matching structured data records between heterogeneous databases. A typical application scenario is matching person records in different person registers, which contain structured data about some same persons, but are expressed using different metadata schemas and notations. Using RL, richer global descriptions of persons can be created based on local datasets.

This paper concerns the problem of entity reconciliation and RL of persons in military historical person registers. As a case study, three complementary datasets about some 100 000 Finnish Second World War soldiers in WarSampo [7,10] are considered. A probabilistic record linkage [6] solution for linking person records is presented, as well as promising evaluation results. The key idea is

E. Blomqvist et al. (Eds.): SEMANTiCS 2020, LNCS 12378, pp. 118–126, 2020.
https://doi.org/10.1007/978-3-030-59833-4_8

to assign weights to various comparisons of metadata fields between person registers. The weights can tell us what information is important for disambiguating person records in the military history context.

After the matches between registers are generated, information is aggregated into the actor ontology, which contains the identities and enriched metadata of each person. Integrating the person registers into a single *knowledge graph (KG)* facilitates biographical and prosopographical research [9].

The WarSampo KG is published as open data[1] and is part of the international Linked Open Data Cloud. The WarSampo portal[2] [7] demonstrates the usefulness of the resulting KG integrated from various sources. WarSampo uses Linked Data and the event-based *CIDOC Conceptual Reference Model (CRM)*[3] together as a basis for harmonizing various datasets about Finland in the Second World War. The portal provides nine customized interactive "perspectives" on the data: (war) Events, Persons, Army Units, Places, Magazine Articles, Casualties, Photographs, War Cemeteries, and Prisoners of War. Since its opening in 2015, the WarSampo portal has been used by more than 710 000 end users, corresponding to more than 10% of the population in Finland.

Related Work. Overviews of the RL field are presented in [6,13]. Antolie et al. [1] present a case study of integrating Canadian World War I data from three sources: one of soldiers, one of casualties, and a census dataset, using a series of handcrafted deterministic RL processes. Research use of the resulting longitudinal data is demonstrated. Cunningham [3] presents integrating a World War I veteran military service record with a census database using a deterministic RL process and provides findings of quantitative analysis of the data for historical research.

The Historical Population Register (HPR) of Norway is pursuing to cover the country's whole population in 1800–1964 combining information with RL from church records and censuses [12]. The Links project[4] has similar goals in the Netherlands aiming to reconstruct all nineteenth and early twentieth century families in the Netherlands based on all civil certificates from this period.

2 Data: WarSampo Person Registers

In WarSampo, information about a single person can be found in multiple person registers, each bringing in some new information about the person. The information found from multiple sources can be combined to create a more complete biography of the person. However, it is challenging to reliably say whether two similar looking person records in different registers refer to the same actual person as they contain no common fields with shared unique values.

---

[1] https://doi.org/10.5281/zenodo.3431121.
[2] http://sotasampo.fi/en/.
[3] http://cidoc-crm.org.
[4] Cf. the project homepage https://iisg.amsterdam/en/hsn/projects/links and research papers at https://iisg.amsterdam/en/hsn/projects/links/links-publications.

The military rank and military unit of a soldier are prone to change in time due to promotions or even demotions. There can be different spellings of a name, middle names can be missing, and in Finland many originally foreign surnames were translated into Finnish in the early 20th century. In practise, the same full name can refer to different persons, and different names can refer to the same person. There are currently three different person registers in WarSampo:

1. **Initial Actor Ontology.** The ontology containing 5600 people, and also military units, has been created from various data sources which provide varying levels of detail [11]. For most of the people there is rich biographical metadata, e.g. a person's full name, the dates and places of birth and death, occupation, and dates of promotions during the military career. However, in some cases the level of detail is not sufficient for disambiguation, e.g., only a surname and military rank may be known.

2. **Register of Military Death in the Finnish Wars 1939–1945.** The register contains 94 700 death records (DR) [8], depicting the status of the person at the time of his/her death. The spreadsheet source data contains detailed information about the known Finnish persons who perished in WW2. There are 32 columns of structured information about each person, with each cell having a single literal value.

3. **Register of the Prisoners of War in Soviet Union 1939–1945.** The register contains 4200 prisoner records (PR) [9], depicting the status of persons at the time when they were captured. It was published in WarSampo on November 2019. The spreadsheet source data contains mostly very detailed information about each known Finnish prisoner of war. The spreadsheet contains 45 columns of information about each person, gathered from, e.g., various archives. Often a single cell contains multiple values corresponding to information in different sources, following a pre-defined cell formatting. Most of the cells contain well-formed literal values, like the municipality of birth, military rank, and date of returning from captivity.

3   Method: Linking Person Records

The WarSampo KG is built from source datasets using a repeatable data transformation pipeline [10]. In this approach, the domain experts maintain the primary data in the original native format, i.e., typically spreadsheets. When a source dataset is updated, the pipeline can be used to easily recreate the whole KG with the updated data.

The pipeline transforms the source spreadsheets of DRs and PRs into RDF, mapping the columns to RDF properties, with possibly multiple values per property. Automatic probabilistic entity linking processes then link the records to the WarSampo domain ontologies of military ranks, units, occupations, people, and places. This *semantic reconciliation* improves the interoperability [4] of the person registers. If the related domain ontologies are updated, the whole integration process can be redone to account for the changes in the probabilistic entity linking.

The person record linkage is performed after linking the metadata values to domain ontologies. This is challenging because of heterogeneity of the metadata schemas, ambiguous metadata annotations, temporal changes, and errors in the data. Approximate similarity matches of metadata fields is often useful when working with noisy historical person records [1].

The two record linkage scenarios that are needed to tackle for integrating data from all three person registers are:

RL1. DRs (94 700 person records) linked with the initial actor ontology (5600 persons)

RL2. PRs (4200 person records) linked with the actor ontology enriched with the DRs (99 667 persons)

The first developed solution, applied in both scenarios, was a deterministic (or rule-based) RL, in which all person pairs were compared with each other, and scored based on a pre-defined handcrafted formula. This was manually evaluated to provide at least satisfactory results (precision estimated to be at least 0.9), but as the datasets were being updated and the ontologies evolving, manually maintaining the scoring formula was decided to be not sustainable.

The second solution is to use probabilistic RL [6], with a logistic regression-based machine learning implementation employing the Dedupe Python library [5]. Results from the previous solution are used as training data, consisting of 216 matches for *RL1* and 1234 matches for *RL2*. Of these, the ones close to the match acceptance threshold were manually validated to be correct. Person instances or person records with only 3 or less metadata fields for the RL are ignored as too ambiguous in the linking process. The RL solution[5] is open-source, and is used in the transformation processes of the DRs[6] and the PRs[7]. A run of the probabilistic RL process completes within a few hours in both of the scenarios on an average desktop computer.

The scoring of possible pairs between the PRs and the persons already integrated to WarSampo, i.e., initial actor ontology and DRs, are performed using the comparisons of properties shown in Table 1. The weighted sum of the individual comparisons is used as a confidence that a given pair of records is a match, i.e., that it refers to the same real world person. If the weighted sum is above a given, manually fine-tuned threshold, the records are considered a match. The comparisons of type *string* use hyper-parameter optimization to find the best performing string comparison for the values, e.g., Jaro-Winkler. The *intersection* comparisons compare the one or more URI values of both records to see if there is a matching URI or not. The *date* comparisons measure the distance of two dates based on CIDOC CRM time-spans, which have separate earliest and latest dates. The *numerical* comparison measures the distance of numerical values.

To address temporal changes in a person's military rank and the observed variance in the use of different private level ranks, a comparison based on the

---

[5] https://github.com/SemanticComputing/warsa-linkers.

[6] https://github.com/SemanticComputing/Casualty-linking.

[7] https://github.com/SemanticComputing/WarPrisoners.

Table 1. Used metadata comparisons between the registers for the probabilistic RL.

Property	Comparison type	Binary/Continuous variable
Given names	String	Continuous
Family name	String	Continuous
Municipality of birth	Intersection	Binary
Date of birth [earliest]	Date	Continuous
Date of birth [latest]	Date	Continuous
Date of death [earliest]	Date	Continuous
Date of death [latest]	Date	Continuous
Municipality of death	Intersection	Binary
Activity end	Date	Binary
Military rank	Intersection	Binary
Military rank level	Numerical	Continuous
Military unit	Intersection	Binary
Occupation	Intersection	Binary

comparative level of a rank is used. This also addresses the rather permanent separation between enlisted ranks and commissioned officers.

Aggregating Personal Information. After the links of records between registers are generated, information is aggregated into the actor ontology, which contains the identities and basic metadata of each person, with a data model based on CIDOC CRM. New person instances are created in the actor ontology for the records that did not match any existing person and existing person instances are enriched with new information. The person records are modeled as instances of CIDOC CRM's document class, which are linked to the person instances in the actor ontology.

4　Results and Evaluation

The record linkage scenario *RL1* results in 620 DRs linked to matching people in the 5611 pre-existing person instances, corresponding to 11% of the people in the actor ontology. For the remaining 94 056 DRs, new person instances are created.

The *RL2* scenario results in 1255 person records linked to matching people in the 99 667 pre-existing person instances, corresponding to 30% of the PRs. Of the matches, 1234 already exist in the training data as the initial deterministic solution was already quite successful in matching the records based on an early version of the prisoner register. For 2945 PRs, new person instances are created in the actor ontology.

Comparison Weights. The learned comparison weights depict what information is useful for disambiguating person records in the military history context. The weights of the comparisons vary a little as new runs on updated data are done, but their general magnitude is stable. For the newest WarSampo data transformation, the comparison weights in the *RL2* scenario in descending importance order are: family name (2.3), municipality of birth (2.0), given names (1.4), date of birth earliest (1.2), birth date latest (1.2), military rank (1.0), occupation (0.9), military unit (0.8), military rank level (0.8), municipality of death (0.4). The remaining comparisons have weight under 0.1.

Names, municipality of birth and date of birth are intuitively very important personal details defining a persons identity. As the date of birth is split into two comparisons, it's overall importance can be summed up to 2.4, making it the single most important metadata field. The summed weight of military rank, 1.8, is higher than that of given names. Military unit is also important, nearly as much as a person's occupation. Occupation of soldiers probably have not changed during the war, but what is considered a persons occupation might vary depending on the situation and accountant.

Linking Quality. Due to the mostly rich data of each person contained in the person registers, manual evaluation of found links is usually possible, by examining the data in detail. This enables estimating the RL precision. Recall evaluation however, would need manual inspection of a very high amount of possible pairs, of which some have very little information. Also, the DRs are known to contain plenty of errors. Hence, it is in many cases difficult to confidently determine the true negative results, i.e., the cases where there is no match, which is crucial for the recall evaluation. However, manual inspection of matches that almost met the matching threshold were either ambiguous or false, suggesting that the recall is adequate.

The precision of the record linkage in both scenarios *RL1* and *RL2* was manually evaluated to be 1.00, based on randomly selecting 150 links from the total of 620 links for *RL1*, and 200 links from the total of 1397 links for the *RL2*. The information on the person records and the person instances was compared, and all of the linked records were interpreted to be depicting the same actual persons with high confidence.

Using the Aggregated Information. The aggregation of information from multiple sources provides more full soldier biographies than when using individual sources. For example, the PRs fill a gap that would otherwise exist for each of the captured soldiers by providing, e.g., detailed information about their movements between prison camps.

There are also person related documents that are linked to the person instances or their military units, i.e., a large collection of wartime photographs, hand-written digitized war diaries, and war veteran magazine articles. These easily provide further information for people studying for example the war paths of their relatives.

The Persons perspective of the WarSampo portal uses the aggregated person instances and information directly from the linked person records to create a unified view of all the information of each person, in a sense creating a "homepage" for them.[8] In addition to showing the aggregated information, links are provided to related documents as well as related military units and people.

5   Discussion

This paper presented the probabilistic record linkage process used in WarSampo to integrate heterogeneous person registers into a reconciled KG, which uses training data created by a simpler deterministic RL solution. The solution is capable of automatically handling updates in the person registers or related domain ontologies. The aggregated information can be used for, e.g., biographical or prosopographical research by historians, or for study and exploration by interested citizens.

The weights of different metadata field comparisons, assigned using logistic regression, shed light on what metadata fields are useful in disambiguating person references in the military history context. Military rank and military unit are both important person details when determining the identity of a person depicted in a person record.

The data is published openly on SPARQL endpoint and on the WarSampo portal, where anyone can evaluate the links between different person records as they are modeled as separate resources in the data and information sources are shown to users. The Persons perspective of the portal displays all information about a single person in the KG. The Casualties and Prisoners perspectives provide faceted search and visualizations to explore, study, and analyze the DRs and PRs, respectively. In the future, a similar perspective for the aggregated person instances would be useful, where a user can conduct similar prosopographical analysis over all the persons.

The solution is scalable and can be further used to integrate more person registers into WarSampo. For considerably larger person registers, a blocking strategy [2] based on the metadata values should be adopted to reduce the number of comparisons. The presented approach is applicable also to other studies integrating historical person registers. A simple deterministic RL process can be useful for creating training data for a probabilistic RL process in similar scenarios where the process needs to be able to handle regular data updates automatically.

In the future, a register of the soldiers who survived the war would be a valuable addition to WarSampo, providing the means to study subjects such as what affects the soldiers' likelihood of surviving the war.

Acknowledgements. Our work has been funded by the Association for Cherishing the Memory of the Dead of the War, Teri-Säätiö, Open Science and Research Initiative of the Finnish Ministry of Education and Culture, the Finnish Cultural Foundation, and the Academy of Finland.

---

[8] Cf. an example person "homepage" at https://www.sotasampo.fi/en/persons/person_65.

References

1. Antonie, L., Gadgil, H., Grewal, G., Inwood, K.: Historical data integration, a study of WWI canadian soldiers. In: 2016 IEEE 16th International Conference on Data Mining Workshops (ICDMW), pp. 186–193. IEEE (2016)
2. Christen, P.: Data Matching: Concepts and Techniques for Record Linkage, Entity Resolution, and Duplicate Detection. Springer, Berlin (2012)
3. Cunningham, A.: After "it's over over there": using record linkage to enable the reconstruction of World War I veterans' demography from soldiers' experiences to civilian populations. Hist. Methods J. Quant. Interdisc. Hist. **51**, 1–27 (2018)
4. Gal, A., Anaby-Tavor, A., Trombetta, A., Montesi, D.: A framework for modeling and evaluating automatic semantic reconciliation. VLDB J. Int. J. Very Large Data Bases **14**(1), 50–67 (2005)
5. Gregg, F., Eder, D.: Dedupe (2019). https://github.com/dedupeio/dedupe
6. Gu, L., Baxter, R., Vickers, D., Rainsford, C.: Record linkage: Current practice and future directions. CSIRO Mathematical and Information Sciences (2003), cMIS Technical Report No. 03/83
7. Hyvönen, E., et al.: WarSampo data service and semantic portal for publishing linked open data about the second world war history. In: Sack, H., et al. (eds.) ESWC 2016. LNCS, vol. 9678, pp. 758–773. Springer, Cham (2016). https://doi.org/10.1007/978-3-319-34129-3_46
8. Koho, M., Hyvönen, E., Heino, E., Tuominen, J., Leskinen, P., Mäkelä, E.: Linked death—representing, publishing, and using second world war death records as linked open data. In: Blomqvist, E., Hose, K., Paulheim, H., Ławrynowicz, A., Ciravegna, F., Hartig, O. (eds.) ESWC 2017. LNCS, vol. 10577, pp. 369–383. Springer, Cham (2017). https://doi.org/10.1007/978-3-319-70407-4_45
9. Koho, M., Ikkala, E., Hyvönen, E.: Reassembling the lives of finnish prisoners of the second world war on the semantic web. In: Proceedings of the Third Conference on Biographical Data in the Digital Age (BD 2019). CEUR Workshop Proceedings (2019)
10. Koho, M., Ikkala, E., Leskinen, P., Tamper, M., Tuominen, J., Hyvönen, E.: WarSampo knowledge graph: Finland in the second world war as linked open data. Semantic Web – Interoperability, Usability, Applicability (2020). http://semantic-web-journal.net/content/warsampo-knowledge-graph-finland-second-world-war-linked-open-data
11. Leskinen, P., et al.: Modeling and using an actor ontology of second world war military units and personnel. In: d'Amato, C., et al. (eds.) ISWC 2017. LNCS, vol. 10588, pp. 280–296. Springer, Cham (2017). https://doi.org/10.1007/978-3-319-68204-4_27
12. Thorvaldsen, G., Andersen, T., Sommerseth, H.L.: Record linkage in the historical population register for Norway. In: Population Reconstruction, pp. 155–171. Springer, Cham (2015)
13. Winkler, W.E.: Overview of Record Linkage and Current Research Directions. Technical report, U.S. Census Bureau (2006)

Author Index

Arndt, Natanael   19

Bassiliades, Nick   36
Bensmann, Felix   53

De Donato, Renato   70
De Meester, Ben   87
Dietze, Stefan   53
Dimou, Anastasia   87
Dojchinovski, Milan   1

Frey, Johannes   1, 19

Garofalo, Martina   70
Götz, Fabian   19
Gouidis, Filippos   36
Graux, Damien   104

Hellmann, Sebastian   1, 19
Hofer, Marvin   1
Hyvönen, Eero   118

Kern, Dagmar   53
Koho, Mikko   118

Lehmann, Jens   104
Leskinen, Petri   118
Lieber, Sven   87

Malandrino, Delfina   70

Napolitano, Giulio   104

Papenmeier, Andrea   53
Patkos, Theodore   36
Pellegrino, Maria Angela   70
Petta, Andrea   70

Scarano, Vittorio   70
Sejdiu, Gezim   104
Stadler, Claus   104
Streitmatter, Denis   19

Vassiliades, Alexandros   36
Verborgh, Ruben   87

Zapilko, Benjamin   53

Printed in the United States
By Bookmasters